Tumult and Tears

Tumult and Tears

The Story of the Great War Through the Eyes and Lives of its Women Poets

Vivien Newman

PEN & SWORD
HISTORY

First published in Great Britain in 2016 by
Pen & Sword History
an imprint of
Pen & Sword Books Ltd
47 Church Street
Barnsley
South Yorkshire
S70 2AS

ISBN 9781783831470

A CIP catalogue record for this book is
available from the British Library

Typeset in Ehrhardt by
Replika Press Pvt Ltd, India
Printed and bound in England
By CPI Group (UK) Ltd, Croydon, CR0 4YY

Pen & Sword Books Ltd incorporates the imprints of Pen & Sword
Archaeology, Atlas, Aviation, Battleground, Discovery, Family History,
History, Maritime, Military, Naval, Politics, Railways, Select, Social History,
Transport, True Crime and Claymore Press, Frontline Books, Leo Cooper,
Praetorian Press, Remember When, Seaforth Publishing and Wharncliffe.

For a complete list of Pen & Sword titles please contact
PEN & SWORD BOOKS LIMITED
47 Church Street, Barnsley, South Yorkshire, S70 2AS, England
E-mail: enquiries@pen-and-sword.co.uk

Contents

Dedication

This book is for the Chelmsford Adult Community College English Literature A-Level students who, in 1996, humoured their tutor and studied women's war poetry, particularly Keith Dolan who reluctantly decided to give poetry a chance and continues to do so, and Clare Russell who still listens while we walk – as she has done for nineteen years.

Thanks are due to:

Jen Newby, formerly of Pen & Sword, who greeted the suggestion of an anthology of women's war poetry with such enthusiasm. Her meticulous editing has eliminated many faults – those that remain are my own.

My daughters Rosalind and Elizabeth have continued to indulge their 'Funny Mummy' and have succeeded in never appearing bored by women's war poetry. John Connell-Smith, Debbie Deboltz, Warrant Officer Christopher Earl and Lucinda Semeraro have all achieved a similar feat.

Frances Hall – another of those first students – frequently ferrets out World War One newspaper snippets which are always fascinating.

Dr Vicky Holmes for taking on the task of compiling the index at the eleventh hour – such help at sort notice was invaluable. That this book has seen the light of day owes much to her.

Maria Weiss rose to the challenge of following a contemporary pattern and knitting 'twin socks the Anzac way'. The end result would have been as warmly welcomed by its lucky Great War recipient as by the current one.

Professor Pam Cox of the University of Essex who so many years ago believed that there was a story behind women's war poetry and guided my telling it.

Finally, as always, my thanks and love to Ivan Newman. Despite living with 500 women poets for more than two decades, he is still able to ask probing questions about them and their work and point out the flaws in my arguments.

Abbreviations

AFFW	American Fund for French Wounded
AMS	Army Medical Service
APO	Army Post Office
ASC	Army Service Corps
BEF	British Expeditionary Force
CCS	Casualty Clearing Station
CWGC	Commonwealth War Graves Commission
DORA	Defence of the Realm Act
FANY	First Aid Nursing Yeomanry
KIA	Killed in Action
QAIMNS	Queen Alexandra Imperial Military Nursing Service
QAIMNS(R)	Queen Alexandra Imperial Military Nursing Service (Reserve)
QMAAC	Queen Mary Auxiliary Army Corps (formerly WAAC)
RAMC	Royal Army Medical Corps
SWH	Scottish Women's Hospital for Foreign Service
TFNS	Territorial Forces Nursing Service
VAD	Voluntary Aid Detachment
WAAC	Women's Auxiliary Army Corps (became QMAAC)
WLA	Women's Land Army
WRAF	Women's Royal Air Force
WRNS	Women's Royal Naval Service
YMCA	Young Men's Christian Association

Introduction

'Women's war poetry'?

In September 1996, I was teaching A-Level English Literature at my local Adult Community College. The syllabus had recently changed and I told my new class of eager, predominantly female, adult students that we were going to study an anthology of women's war poetry. Expecting enthusiasm, I was taken aback by the sea of disbelieving faces that surrounded me. The women surreptitiously looked at each other and then a brave soul, acting as self-designated spokesperson, echoed, "Women's war poetry?" The question mark was audible.

On behalf of her colleagues, she sought to put me right, "Women didn't write poetry about or during the First World War. And what can women tell us about war anyway?" Another student added, " 'The War Poets'," this time the capital letters were audible, "were Rupert Brooke, Wilfred Owen, Siegfried Sassoon, Edward Thomas. They were 'There' " – another audible capital letter. "We'd like to study *them*, please."

I stood my ground. This was the poetry text I had selected to study and study it we would. I told myself that my own enthusiasm for women's poetry as well as my love of history, in particular the history of the First World War, would win the students round.

During the first session, we watched the BBC documentary *The Roses of No Man's Land*, commissioned to commemorate the, then recent, eightieth anniversary of the Battle of the Somme. Mesmerized by the harrowing eye-witness accounts of these now very elderly ladies who had served as nurses during the Great War, the class sat in stunned silence as the final credits rolled. It was obvious that these nurses had been in the midst of the blood, the suffering and the horror that up until then had been accepted as the masculine preserve of the War.

A few of the students began thumbing through their anthologies, wondering if maybe a nurse had written a poem. One woman found one, she nudged her neighbour. The mood of the class altered dramatically. Perhaps women poets <u>did</u> have something to say about war. Soon they wanted to know more. Who were these women, what sort of backgrounds did they come from, what education had they received, how old were they, and were there more women war poets than the seventy-nine in the anthology we were studying? Were they writing about their own experiences? Were the poems, other than those written by the nurses, 'true'?

From having initially felt that the students were rather humouring me in my choice of text, it soon became obvious that they were as enthralled as I was. I tried to keep one step ahead of the class but soon realized that I was unable to answer many of their often probing questions, not because I wasn't making the effort to find the answers but because, quite simply, the answers were nowhere to be found. It became obvious that we were only glimpsing the tip of a poetic iceberg. Submerged beneath it was a body of under-researched, indeed unresearched women's literary history – and it appeared increasingly likely that I would have to do the research myself.

One of my first discoveries was that of the well over 2,000 British poets whose work was published during the First World War, more than a quarter were women. Initially this figure seemed amazing and then it became obvious that if the war that lasted from August 1914 to November 1918 had truly been a 'Total War' (in which all of a country's resources are mobilised towards the war effort), then women would also have written about it.

Although, with one notable exception, women did not bear arms, they were naturally affected by the waves of patriotism, excitement, resignation, despair, grief and finally muted relief that swept the nation for four long years. If war poetry is a response to intense emotions, it would have been deeply surprising if women had not written poetry. This was a point that seemed to have escaped most literary critics in the 1990s and who even today have a tendency to dismiss women poets as at worst irrelevant and at best peripheral.

The shibboleth of gender is such that in wartime women's views and voices are considered secondary to war's main business – and its poeticization – namely the killing of males by males. Yet, in terms of subject matter women's poetry is often broader than men's, reflecting that fact that warfare involves far more than writing about the trenches and the camaraderie of those who live and die in battle.

Another surprising discovery was poetry's commercial value. During and immediately after the First World War, anthologies featuring men and women war poets were reprinted multiple times, some 42,000 copies of one American compilation, George Herbert Clarke's *A Treasury of War Poetry*, were printed. National and local newspapers across the English-speaking world had a voracious appetite for poetry. Association magazines and local works journals published verse. Jobbing printers produced poems as broadsides and many of these, like anthologies, were sold to raise funds for 'Good Causes' including one that aimed to provide 'beef tea for our soldiers' and another with the charitable purpose of purchasing tobacco.

Poetry was, quite simply, everywhere. At a 1917 meeting of the Poetry Society, Professor George Saintsbury confided in his colleagues that if anybody could be killed by reading poetry, he should have been for, in three years he had read '7 cubic feet' written by both men and women.

Contemporary editors were noticeably gender-blind. To keep poems rolling in, many papers ran weekly competitions offering lucrative financial prizes. Suggested categories ranged from 'the best poem by a poet On Active Service' (a category open to both men and women in uniform) to a poem that could serve as a 'Hymn to be sung in war-time'. Parodies were suggested, as were poems with Latin or Greek tags. Wilfred Owen was far from alone in spotting the possibilities lurking behind 'Dulce et Decorum Est' – at least four women poets did too and I have lost track of how many women leapt at the chance to outdo Rudyard Kipling's 'If'.

However, I did not know any of this when I first chose the A-Level text. I had soon begun to feel that ground-breaking as the collection was, the poems appearing in alphabetical order by poet, with little historical context and giving only limited biographical information, placed considerable demands on the reader. Occasionally my students and I struggled as we tried to navigate our poetic way round a particular woman or indeed her gender's war.

I began to dream of compiling a different sort of collection to the slim one we were studying. Mine would take a different approach, in the hope that it would be more accessible, more informative and maybe even more rewarding to read. *Tumult and Tears* is the result of that dream and it is indeed very different to the one those initially reluctant students opened twenty years ago, although a few of the poems appear in both.

This anthology presents readers with a wide range of women's poetry, and places it within the context of the War, be this in a general sense or the ways in which the War was impacting upon the individual woman's life. From the outset, my guiding principle was what the piece might tell us about the reality of the War for the poet – and by extension other women, rather than the intrinsic literary 'value' of the poem. Another, equally important aim was to give readers a sense of the sweep of the poetry, both in subject matter and also poetic 'skill'. Some of the poems included are undeniably little more than ditties – albeit heartfelt ones; a few are amongst the finest in the English language.

Finally and crucially, because I am above all a social historian, I wanted readers to have the opportunity to get to know the poet in terms of her social and educational background, age, war service and even, where possible, glimpse her post-war world. All but the last of these factors inform her poetry, although occasionally the future she anticipates for herself informs it as well. The poets' biographies and information about their printing houses, which comprise the second section, are integral to the anthology – and, unlike the poems, these are arranged in alphabetical order.

To help readers to gain an understanding of women's war poetry in general, the poems are grouped in thematic chapters, each has sufficient cultural/historical background to help readers understand why such poems were written. The aim was to show twenty-first century readers that, just like women's contribution to the Allied Victory in 1918, women's war poetry is integral to the genre and not just a sideshow.

Having selected the poems and the chapter themes, I began detective work relating to the poets. Using information contained in local, national and international newspapers and archives including the Red Cross database for VAD nurses (still a work in progress; in July 2015 volunteers had digitalised extant records up to the letter L), census and other official records, some poets emerged from the shadows. Of course, a minority such as VAD Vera Brittain are already relatively well-known; the majority, however, enjoyed, at most, a brief moment of fame when their poem or collection of poems was published and, for the lucky few, even reviewed in publications ranging from the poet's local paper to the *Times Literary Supplement.*

There were occasional Eureka moments, when cracking a poem's code helped to unravel the poet's personal history and this has even led to contacts and friendships. On one occasion family members of one poet (Alexandra Grantham) were discovered in New Zealand. Although they were aware of her existence, they knew nothing about her truly extraordinary war story. Such moments have been rare but the satisfaction when they occur is immense.

Yet, despite intensive research, some poets remain obstinately in the shadows. While the individual's life may be shrouded in mystery, her poem casts light on her war. Thus, we may never know who Paula Hudd was, but we know that she was outraged by war being waged upon children, whilst the periodical or indeed publisher with which a poet chose to publish her poem may give a clue to her political leanings, educational background and even financial status.

As you join me in discovering these women's lives through their poetry, I hope that you derive as much pleasure from reading their poems and finding out about their wartime stories as I have had.

Dr Vivien Newman,
Chelmsford 2015

Chapter 1

When 'Pierrot Goes Forward, What of Pierrette?'

When Great Britain declared war on Germany in the dying hours of 4 August 1914, many of the 27.6 million British women – and indeed women from across the combatant nations – asked themselves a key question. What was a woman's role in wartime?

A British man, if he were aged between eighteen and forty-one, could immediately offer his services to the Armed Forces but, apart from the tiny numbers of professional nurses, no obvious role appeared for women to fulfil. Although some women had professional training and expertise that the nation would, in due course, realise it needed, in the early days there was little for most women to do. What would happen to them in wartime?

This gulf between men and women's wartime roles is perfectly summed up by American poet Gabrielle Elliot.

PIERROT GOES TO WAR

In the sheltered garden pale beneath the moon,
(Drenched with swaying fragrance, redolent with June!)
There, among the shadows, someone lingers yet –
Pierrot, the lover, parts from Pierrette.

Bugles, bugles, bugles, blaring down the wind,
Sound the flaming challenge – *Leave your dreams behind!*
Come away from the shadows, turn your back on June –
Pierrot, go forward to face the golden noon.

In the muddy trenches, black and torn and still,
(How the charge swept over, to break against the hill!)
Huddled in the shadows, boyish figures lie –
They whom Death, saluting, called upon to die.

Bugles, ghostly bugles, whispering down the wind –
Dreams too soon are over, gardens left behind.
Only shadows linger, for love does not forget –
Pierrot goes forward – but what of Pierrette?

Gabrielle Elliot

'And we wept and watched you go': Saying Good-bye

In August 1914, Great Britain had a standing army of under a million men. Battalions on home service, supplemented by reservists, were rapidly mustered, forming the vanguard of the British Expeditionary Force. Several poets recorded their thoughts as they watched Britain's first soldiers march off to war.

Katharine Tynan was an eyewitness to the West Kent Regiment's August departure from Dublin. In this poem, she captures the excited public mood as the men left the safety of home shores and headed for the Western Front.

JOINING THE COLOURS
(West Kents, Dublin, August 1914)

There they go marching all in step so gay!
Smooth-cheeked and golden, food for shells and guns.
Blithely they go as to a wedding day,
The mothers' sons.

The drab street stares to see them row on row
On the high tram-tops, singing like the lark.
Too careless-gay for courage, singing they go
Into the dark.

With tin whistles, mouth-organs, any noise,
They pipe the way to glory and the grave;
Foolish and young, the gay and golden boys
Love cannot save.

High heart! High courage! The poor girls they kissed
Run with them: they shall kiss no more, alas!
Out of the mist they stepped–into the mist
Singing they pass.

Katharine Tynan

Another poet who may also have witnessed the departure of the West Kents or one of the other regiments stationed in Dublin, was Winifred Letts. This, one of the earliest war poems published by a woman, appeared on 15 August 1914 in the *Saturday Westminster Gazette*. The narrator sees the heartbreak and helplessness of the women left behind.

THE CALL TO ARMS IN OUR STREET

There's a woman sobs her heart out,
With her head against the door,
For the man that's called to leave her,
— God have pity on the poor!
But it's beat, drums, beat,
While the lads march down the street,
And it's blow, trumpets, blow,
Keep your tears until they go.

There's a crowd of little children
That march along and shout,
For it's fine to play at soldiers
Now their fathers are called out.
So it's beat, drums, beat;
But who'll find them food to eat?
And it's blow, trumpets, blow,
Ah! the children little know.

There's a mother who stands watching
For the last look of her son,
A worn poor widow woman,
And he her only one.
But it's beat, drums, beat,
Though God knows when we shall meet;
And it's blow, trumpets, blow,
We must smile and cheer them so.

There's a young girl who stands laughing,
For she thinks a war is grand,
And it's fine to see the lads pass,
And it's fine to hear the band.
So it's beat, drums, beat,

To the fall of many feet;
And it's blow, trumpets, blow,
God go with you where you go
To the war.

Winifred Letts

In this poem Letts observes those who were watching their men depart. For many women, their initial contact with the disruption and the heartache of war was bidding an agonising farewell to loved ones who were flocking to the colours. This agony lasted throughout the War and poems relating to farewells occur from the opening days.

One of the thousands of women who knew intimately the anguish involved in saying good-bye was Alexandra Grantham. Both her eldest son and her husband were serving officers.

SONNET XIX

War is a time of sacrifice and parting,
Of hard-fought victory o'er mothers' tears,
That when their sons towards far fights are starting,
By the loud train be mirth not moan of fears.

Good wishes, agony of farewell kisses,
As they together for the last time stand –
The green flag waves, the white steam hisses,
Love's last fond greetings waved with trembling hands.

War is a time of death and long good-bye
To home and all its peaceful blessedness;
A time when our travail's dear children lie
Killed or maimed on alien soil; when wickedness
Hate-maddened Christians goads on blood-drenched plain
To mock and crucify their God again.

Alexandra Grantham

However infrequently it may have occurred, men serving on the Western Front did get some home leave, with officers allocated substantially more than other ranks. Inevitably, each period of leave came to an end, with the trauma of saying goodbye needing to be re-negotiated. Evelyn Tollemache, whose two brothers served (and survived), raises an unanswerable question: who suffers most during the final goodbye?

THE LEAVE TRAIN VICTORIA STATION

In the dim morning through vague archways grey
– Where fitful lamplight struggles with the day –
They gather slowly – all too swift have sped
The precious hours of leave. Still must be said
The sad goodbyes, with lips that may not fail –
With smiling eyes – though not a man but dreads
These last few moments more than any hail
Of shrapnel bullets raining overhead.

'Neath the dim arches close in little bands,
Sad wives and mothers with their loved ones stand.
Daring but trivial parting words – may be
"Come back safely again" or "Write to me."
White lipped, dry eyed, they wait and glance above
To where the great clock points its fateful hand,
Half longing, yet with dread to see it move,
These bravest men and women in the land.

Whose names are blazoned not on any Scroll
Of Glorious Victories, nor in any Roll
Of Battle Honours – yet on platforms grey
In early London mornings every day
Are bitterest battles fought and victories gained.
But whether They that go, or Those who stay –
Lips smiling while their hearts break – have attained
The Greater Triumph, God alone can say.

Evelyn Tollemache

Journalist, social historian and household management author Mrs Peel noted that more than one young girl of the time remembered, 'It used to be hateful if one went to see them off by that horrid leave train.' Another who had become engaged during the War, stated, 'I knew what misery was: one was always waiting, and one almost dreaded the "leaves" because of that awful going back again.' The memory of bidding her fiancé farewell, for what would be the last time, remained with Australian-born, Oxford resident Marian Allen, as it did with countless bereaved women.

CHARING CROSS

I went along the river-side today,
Under the railway bridge at Charing Cross,
Where many such as you are swept away
And we are left to wonder at your loss.
The station echoes with your ghostly feet;
Your laughing voices cling about each wall;
You entered gaily from the sunlit street
To pass into the sun again and fall.
The train slid out under the April sky
And London's throbbing heart was left behind;
And many more will follow you to die,
Crossing the silent river, there to find
Host upon host, their comrades glorified,
Saluting them upon the other side.

Marian Allen

It was not only adults who accompanied soldiers to railway stations, countless children did too. Decades later, many who had lived through these moments recalled the agony of waiting for the final whistle to blow and seeing their father disappear, maybe for ever.

TRAIN

Will the train never start?
God, make the train start.

She cannot bear it, keeping up so long;
and he, he no more tries to laugh at her.
He is going.

She holds his two hands now.
Now, she has touch of him and sight of him.
And then he will be gone.
He will be gone.

They are so young.
She stands under the window of his carriage,
and he stands in the window.
They hold each other's hands
across the window ledge.
And look and look,
and know that they may never look again.

The great clock of the station–
how strange it is.
Terrible that the minutes go,
terrible that the minutes never go.

They had walked the platform for so long,
up and down, and up and down–
the platform, in the rainy morning,
up and down, and up and down.

The guard came by, calling,
"Take your places, take your places."

She stands under the window of his carriage,
and he stands in the window.

God, make the train start!
Before they cannot bear it,
make the train start!

God, make the train start!

The three children, there,
in black, with the old nurse,
standing together, and looking, and looking,
up at their father in the carriage window,
they are so forlorn and silent.

The little girl will not cry,
but her chin trembles.
She throws back her head, with its stiff little braid,
and will not cry.

Her father leans down,
out over the ledge of the window,
and kisses her, and kisses her.

She must be like her mother,
and it must be the mother who is dead.
The nurse lifts up the smallest boy,
and his father kisses him,
leaning through the carriage window.

The big boy stands very straight,
and looks at his father,
and looks, and never takes his eyes from him,
And knows that he may never look again.

Will the train never start?
God, make the train start!

The father reaches his hand down from the window,
and grips the boy's hand,
and does not speak at all.

Will the train never start?

He lets the boy's hand go.

Will the train never start?

He takes the boy's chin in his hand,
leaning out through the window,
and lifts the face that is so young, to his.
They look and look,
and know that they may never look again.

Will the train never start?
God, make the train start!

Helen Mackay

For some, saying goodbye in the very public space of a station was too much to bear, even for the wife of a regular army officer who was used to such painful events.

THE FAREWELL

Oh, not tonight beloved – not now, to-night, bid me farewell
Wait, wait, till dawn uprising into sight breaks the dear spell!
There is no night when love's great altar stands bare and reproved,
Just darkness where in each our distant lands we sleep, beloved.
Shall we not gather then one more tomorrow? Ah no, in vain,
Duty, however reckless, may not borrow from Time's domain,
And though I bid you stay I'd have you go, oh heart, my heart!
I need not tell you, you already know. Proudly we part,
Proudly we add our piteous tiny mite to all the grief
Staggering the world for this huge cause of right and high belief,
Though all unknown the meaning of the lust let loose on earth,
Before whose power rises out of dust a world's rebirth.

Perchance we walked too blithely with our peace, reckoned too sure
That all the snares which made for ill should cease, ourselves secure.
We let the Past slip by us without care; we heard in vain
Far echoing sobs of women and the prayer of captive men.
We let our faith turn rotten on the bough; disdained its seed,
Our guilt is measured by the strength of vow made in our need.

But oh, for other ways than by those gates, opening on death,
While Hope in utter silence sits and waits, catching her breath.
By other ways than through that fierce domain of flame and fire,
Where Hell itself sees nothing more to gain or to desire.
All that we dreamed in linking mate with mate, all bliss and love
Tossed to the crucible of warring fate, its strength to prove,
All that we dreamed and planned and haply sought, all smiles and tears,
All loyalty and vows and trust unsought and woman's fears,
Crushed in the Juggernaut of tyranny, of wrath and death,
And Battle's proud and long-drawn agony and simple faith.
Oh I had strength and now I have no more, now you must go,
Nay, do not check me, let my heart be sore, let my tears flow,
Let me be me and not the heroine that others are,
So shall our memory make sure to win and hold one star,

Not ice-bound with the courage of despair, but near and true,
Sobbing out softly all that I may dare from me to you
For neither in the rush of fretting time beating his wings
In vain against the eternal law sublime of ordered things,
Nor yet in silence of the upturned flowers Death sadly reaps,
Constrained to fill the overburdened hours while mercy weeps,
Shall I forget, so you remember there where flaming pure,
Faith's spirit rises through the tortured air, strong to endure.

Only I ask you, bid me not goodbye, here's no such word,
Put your arms round me so, in that last sigh our prayer is heard;
Guard that prayer ever, dearest one, nor grieve, holding our love,
But kiss me long, ere yet you take your leave, night still above:
So shall I keep you enduringly, be with you still,
Climb with you to that topmost destiny, yours to fulfil.

Aimée Byng Scott

Elinor Jenkins captures the agony of the final countdown before bidding farewell, both for he who left and those who remained. Her beloved, near contemporary uncle, Harry (whom this poem is almost certainly about), and her eldest brother, Arthur, would both pass into what she calls 'the silence and the night'; Harry in 1915 and Arthur in 1917.

THE LAST EVENING

ROUND a bright isle, set in a sea of gloom,
We sat together, dining,
And spoke and laughed even as in better times
Though each one knew no other might misdoubt
The doom that marched moment by moment nigher,
Whose couriers knocked on every heart like death,
And changed all things familiar to our sight
Into strange shapes and grieving ghosts that wept.
The crimson-shaded light
Shed in the garden roses of red fire
That burned and bloomed on the decorous limes.
The hungry night that lay in wait without
Made blind, blue eyes against the silver's shining
And waked the affrighted candles with its breath

Out of their steady sleep, while round the room
The shadows crouched and crept.
Among the legions of beleaguering fears,
Still we sat on and kept them still at bay,
A little while, a little longer yet,
And wooed the hurrying moments to forget
What we remembered well,
—Till the hour struck— then desperately we sought
And found no further respite— only tears
We would not shed, and words we might not say.
We needs must know that now the time was come
Yet still against the strangling foe we fought,
And some of us were brave and some
Borrowed a bubble courage nigh to breaking,
And he that went, perforce went speedily
And stayed not for leave-taking.
But even in going, as he would dispel
The bitterness of incomplete good-byes,
He paused within the circle of dim light,
And turned to us a face, lit seemingly
Less by the lamp than by his shining eyes.
So, in the radiance of his mastered fate,
A moment stood our soldier by the gate
And laughed his long farewell —
Then passed into the silence and the night.

Elinor Jenkins

'Check the thoughts that cluster thick': Knitting poems

Having exchanged farewells, many women would wander back to empty homes and try to pick up the semblance of normality, needing above all else to keep their thoughts and fears at bay. It very quickly became apparent that British Army quartermasters were unable to cope with equipping the hundreds of thousands of volunteers that the recruitment drive was bringing forward. Backed by Queen Mary, an appeal was made to the women of England to knit 300,000 pairs of socks by Christmas. They responded.

Soon the country resounded to the click of knitting needles and, like every aspect of the women's war, knitting soon became the stuff of poetry. For many women, knitting – now much mocked but at the time vital to the war effort – was one way of controlling those 'thoughts that cluster thick'.

Knitting poems range from the light-hearted, some penned by children (for children as young as three and four knitted face cloths and simple scarves) to include with the gifts that they sent to the Front, to parodies and sophisticated polished works that use knitting as a metaphor for love, anxiety and grief. This is perhaps best summed up by one young woman who realised as she watched her mother's hands darting along the lines, that 'it's not a sock she's knitting, it's a web of love for him'.

Some children were highly skilled knitters; others simply accepted the necessity of 'Doing Their Bit' however their parents saw fit. Others were eventually allowed to abandon their task, as a mother's enthusiasm sometimes surpassed her child's skill. Young Betsey Jane eventually turns to painting, although her mother, artist and poet Helen Parry Eden, is not convinced that her daughter has inherited her parents' artistic talents – her father was also an artist.

ARS IMMORTALIS

Betsey, when all the stalwarts left
Us women to our tasks befitting,
Your little fingers, far from deft,
Coped for an arduous week with knitting;

And, though the meekness of your hair
Drooped o'er the task, disarmed my strictures,
The Army gained when in despair
You dropped its socks to paint it pictures.

I, knowing well your guileless brush,
Urged that there wanted something subtler
To put Meissonier* to the blush
And snatch the bays from Lady Butler.*

Helen Parry Eden

[Editor:* *Meissonier and Lady Elizabeth Butler were both renowned war artists who famously depicted the Napoleonic Wars. One of Lady Butler's most famous paintings was The Roll Call; she portrayed the pain rather than the glory of war. Poetry by her famous poet sister, Alice Meynell, was widely published throughout the First World War.*]

Some children who were both knitters and amateur poets, like Sophie Presley Glemby, were keen to record their patriotic endeavours.

MY SOCKS

I am only a little girl
But I am doing my bit
By helping the grown-ups knit socks,
And God grant my prayer
To watch our boys Over There
And bring them home safe
To all longing mothers, fathers, sisters, brothers,
That is a child's prayer.

Sophie Presley Glemby

Irrespective of the poem's theme – or indeed the poet's age – parodies were a popular verse form during the War. These supplied the aspiring poet with a ready-made structure and rhyme pattern. There is no shortage of parodies relating to almost every aspect of women's work and knitting is no exception; unsurprisingly, Mary and her lamb were a popular starting point.

MARY HAD A LITTLE LAMB

Mary had a little lamb
Its fleece was quite expensive,
It followed her to school one day,
And came home feeling pensive.

The little maids at school that day
Forgot their sums and letters.
They pulled the wool all off its back
And knit it into sweaters.

Anonymous

The fate of Mary's lamb would have struck a chord with Australian sheep. When knitters in New South Wales found themselves unable to source sufficient wool, they turned to New South Wales's own immediately available resource: sheep. According to the handbook of the Australia Comforts Fund, 'knitting direct from the fleece' contributed materially to the ever-growing pile of socks.

Although mufflers, sweaters and other comforts were greatly appreciated by the soldiers, socks were needed above all. Not only did Kitchener call for them, nurses at the various fronts pleaded for them, as woollen socks could quite literally save a soldier's feet and ultimately his life. The most skilled knitters were encouraged to knit two socks at once and in Australia patterns were available for those who wished to double their output.

TIME WILL WIN – KNIT A TWIN

In days of the not so long ago
Twin boys played round the bungalow.
For us it was mend and darn and sew;
Little toes soon wear through, you know.
There are no boys in the cottage now.
One in France, one at the chaser's bow,
Beg for socks, so our needles obey,
Twin socks are knit, the Anzac way.

Mrs Mary K Gibbons

[Editor: *A very talented modern day Swiss knitter undertook this task using an original World War One pattern and confirmed its complexity.*]

Not all knitting poems were light-hearted. Jessie Pope is aware of the therapeutic benefits of knitting.

SOCKS

Shining pins that dart and click
In the fireside's sheltered peace
Check the thoughts the cluster thick –
20 plain and then decrease.

He was brave – well, so was I –
Keen and merry, but his lip
Quivered when he said good-bye –
Purl the seam-stitch, purl and slip.

Never used to living rough,
Lots of things he'd got to learn;
Wonder if he's warm enough –
Knit 2, catch 2, knit, turn.

Hark! The paper-boys again!
Wish that shout could be suppressed;
Keeps one always on the strain –
Knit off 9, and slip the rest.

Wonder if he's fighting now,
What he's done an' where he's been;
He'll come out on top somehow –
Slip 1, knit 2, purl 14.

Jessie Pope

If for some knitters their handwork helped keep thoughts at bay, for others it was a way of connecting with those at the Front. There is something deeply personal about making a garment that a loved one is going to wear next to their skin.

TO MY MOTHER

On flash her fingers busily, and swift the pattern grows,
And fall the stitches evenly in neatly rounded rows.
And softer eyes are smiling, but they never see at all
The clumsy thread unwinding from the dull, grey worsted ball.
Her shining needles glitter with a thousand mystic gleams –
It isn't *wool* she's weaving there, it's a gossamer of dreams.

A rosy dream of fights forgot and clouded skies serene,
A white, white dream of honour and a spirit brave and clean.
A thrill of pride, half-fearful, for the strength to do and dare,
A tender little blessing and a quiet little prayer.
And in and out she weaves them from a heart with hope a brim –
It's not a *sock* she's making, it's a web of love for *him*.

Anne Page

Women from across the combatant nations all knitted. Initially, American women had sent socks to Allied soldiers, but when their own nation entered the War in 1917, American knitters and knitting poems proliferated. Eager to encourage both a supply of socks for the boys at the Front (a US Red Cross poster urged citizens to 'Knit Their Bit' as 'Our Boys Need Sox') and contributions to its popular poetry column, *The New York Sun* offered prizes of balls of wool for the three winning poems published every week and also printed the next ten a gaining an 'honourable mention'.

The winning poems were collected by the paper's Arts Editor Harry Dounce and published as *Sock Songs* (1919). The foreword informed readers that Dounce 'was a tireless platform missionary of the patriotic knitter propaganda'. The London *Daily Graphic* also offered prizes for the best knitting poems but these were never collected post-war.

Like their European sisters, American women gained comfort from knitting together. For those without sons, knitting and poeticizing knitting gave them a vicarious entry into the War, as several poems by the childless Mrs Amy W Eggleston demonstrate.

UNTITLED

I must accept my woman's fate
To stay at home – and wait
Wait – though keen anguish clutches at my heart,
Wait – while busily I do my part.
When messenger or post stops at the gate
I see but a dread harbinger of fate.
Still must I knit my socks –
And wait.

Amy Eggleston

Just as women's wartime knitting has, for the better part of a century, received unjustified derision, so the plethora of knitting poems have generally been overlooked. Yet they provide insights into women's coping strategies, into the webs of love they were seeking to weave with their own or another woman's beloved and they suggest a fellowship between women who knit.

Contemporary poems and accounts show that knitting was ageless and classless. According to social commentator and co-director of women's services at the Ministry of Food, Mrs Peel, 'We knitted in trains and trams, in parks and parlours.' It is unlikely that Kitchener had foreseen quite such enthusiasm when he issued his rallying call to needles. By November 1914, in Great Britain alone a total of 970,000 pairs of socks had been produced for the nation's serving men and equally staggering numbers were produced by Australian, Canadian, and New Zealand women and also Americans.

It is therefore hardly surprising that while, as in the words of a contemporary song, the women of England and the Empire 'got on with their knitting', this frenzy was recorded in poetry.

'My Hymn of Hate': Hoarders, food controllers and shopkeepers

Even before war was declared, some members of parliament had expressed anxiety that an outbreak of hostilities would lead to inflated food prices, hoarding and shortages. On 11 August 1914, the government moved to control food prices – although many honourable gentlemen were not convinced that the nation's food supplies would ever be seriously threatened. Such optimism was misplaced. Great Britain was overly-dependent upon imported food and, as German submarine warfare began to bite, thousands of tons of foodstuffs were sent to the bottom of the ocean along with merchant ships and their crews.

As shortages became increasingly visible, Mrs Pember-Reeves, the Ministry of Food's Director of Women's Services, announced, in 1917, that food was 'largely a woman's question', claiming that 'it was for the women to do the trick' of resolving the situation. However, long before she appeared on the scene the majority of women had become only too aware of the food crisis afflicting the nation. Hours spent queuing to purchase basic provisions had, from very early on, become part of their wartime lives.

Poems abound featuring food shortages, some of the unappetising recipes concocted by wartime cooks, and 'the hoarder', amongst the most hated figures of the British Home Front.

THE HOARDER

Every day she haunts the grocer
Buying sugar pound by pound;
One day this shop – then another –
Just where'er it may be found.

To herself she fondly murmurs,
As her store she eyes with pride,
"When my neighbours have no sugar,
I'll have plenty put aside."

"I and mine can eat in safety,
With my daily growing store;
While my neighbours not so careful
Will their empty tins deplore."

Does she think for just one instant,
Of our sailors on the foam –
Think for just one fleeting second
What they bear – for us at home?

No one who is truly British, –
British both in name and heart –
Would of self think, at this crisis,
For 'tis but a coward's part.

M Stone

If hoarders were seen as unpatriotic, shopkeepers who favoured some customers over others also met with opprobrium. Black markets inevitably thrived and rumours as to where certain foods might be available also flourished – leading to anger when they proved false or the shopkeeper uncooperative.

THE RETALIATORS

"It's no good telling me,
        I don't believe you!
I know you've got some.
        Yes, in stock.
        Sold out?
        Oh, you unblushing liar!
My cook's neighbour's aunt
Bought some this very day
And in this very shop.
I know it for a fact.
The milkman's second cousin
        Saw her do it,
And less than half an hour ago.
You've hidden it away!
        I know your tricks,

Reserving it for customers
You want to favour.
But I won't be done,
I'll go at once and fetch a policeman,
He'll soon show you up,
Hunt out the secret store,
He'll get you fined,
And put in prison too, I hope,
You holder up of stocks,
   You shameless liar!"

Helen Hamilton

Citizens were urged to cut thinner slices of bread, use leftovers in imaginative ways and weigh every morsel of food. One nine-year-old who just gave her name as Phyllis, found the latter, at least, a blessing:

SCALES AND EXERCISE

In the days of peace the Mater seemed to have a heart of stone
Every morning for an hour she made us play
The five-finger exercises till the tears would dim your eyes.
But now that all our food we have to weigh,
That disgusting old piano is severely left alone;
After breakfast mother very seldom fails
To say 'Now then dears, you know
I should like to see you go
To the kitchen for your practice with the scales.'

As the situation deteriorated, 'meatless days' (Wednesdays) and sugar cards were introduced, while consumers were constantly urged to 'Eat Less Food'. In 1917, the bread allowance was cut to 4lbs (1.8kg) per person per week and rationing was mooted. Food Control Committees were set up in the summer of 1917 to try to ensure ever-decreasing supplies were more equitably distributed. Inspectors were appointed; Food Controllers, whose directives were supposedly sacrosanct, had the power to prosecute offenders. They also found their way into unflattering poetry:

MY HYMN OF HATE

I hate Food Controllers;
They play cards - sugar cards -
Which give me a head-ache but no sugar.
They command me not to eat bacon,
Then raise the price to make sure I don't.
Even in their sleep they murmur "Eat less bread,"
And every time I taste it I wish I could.

I hate Food Controllers:
They make long speeches about butter;
And it worries me trying to remember where I saw it last.
They tell me that the eggs I buy ought to go to the wounded.
But I don't send them
Because
I cannot afford the gas masks that should accompany them.

I hate Food Controllers:
They are too wise;
They say tea-drinking is a habit which must be broken,
And when I have stood in a queue from Monday morning –
And someone has stood on me –
Until Saturday night,
When I get two ounces that the grocer has found when he swept the shop,
I know they are right.

I hate Food Controllers:
They are too gallant,
They are always saying "Ladies First,"
And then they smile when they are being photographed.

Beryl Swift

Garden associations also entered the fray. They, like the press, were eager to convince gardeners that they too could do their bit for the nation's tables. Landowners from the King and Queen to suburban residents were urged to plough up their flower gardens in favour of food production. Prime Minister Lloyd George patriotically surrendered the tennis courts attached to the grounds of Brynawdon Criccieth, his North Wales residence, and according to *Graphic* of 16 June 1917, brides sacrificed floral bouquets in favour of vegetables!

Sybil Bristowe was amongst the countless who heeded the gardening advice. She accepts that to many with more luxurious spaces, in peacetime her Maida Vale 'London Garden 1914' would seem merely a 'tiny square/Of bordered green/And gravel brown', to her it was 'an oasis of hope'. Its 1918 appearance, however, provides a different type of hope.

MY GARDEN 1918

> Such was my garden once, a Springtide hope of flowers,
> All rosy pink or violet or blue
> Or yellow gold with sunflakes on the dew.
> Now in their place a Summer garden tower
> Of green-leaved artichokes and turnip tops,
> Of peas and parsnips, sundry useful crops.
> – But even vegetables must have little flowers.

Public spaces as well as private gardens were used for food production and many different uniformed services, from Girl Guides to the khaki-clad members of the Women's Volunteer Reserve, tried to comply with government advice to 'Grow More Food'.

KENT 'A' GARDEN

> In Warwick Park at Tunbridge Wells
> There was a field o'ergrown
> With grass and thistles, weeds and stones;
> And rubbish there was thrown.
>
> We got permission for our Corps
> To dig this up and sow it
> With vegetables, fruits and herbs
> To give help where we owe it.
>
> The ground was hard, so very hard,
> And Oh our backs were aching!
> But with a will we set to work
> At digging, hoeing, raking.

And when the rain poured down we thought
Of those who fought the Boches,
In muddy trench, on tossing sea –
We worked in mackintoshes.

And some there were who looked with dread
On slugs and worms so squirmy
One said "oh put me on a job
That isn't quite so wormy!"

And then one day we looked with pride
Upon the green tops showing.
Our seed potatoes had come up,
And healthy shoots were growing.

God bless our Navy on the sea,
And give us power to aid them.
Our wounded too, in hospitals
We long with gifts to lade them.

And if our garden prospers well,
And we grow things to eat,
We'll send them to the hospitals
And to our gallant Fleet.

M Stone, Orderly Sergeant, Kent 'A' Company

Despite the best efforts of gardeners and the Women's Volunteer Reserve, such measures proved insufficient to keep starvation at bay and in 1917 a uniformed female army appeared on the land (poetry produced by its members is considered in Chapter Four).

By the time the food crisis had really begun to make itself felt, another shortage had already hit the nation and once again, women were directly affected.

'Working on Munitions to help to win the war'

Although the wartime manufacture of munitions has come to be closely associated with ordnance-making, women were involved in all aspects of equipping the armed forces. They were employed in very considerable numbers in factories which manufactured rations, sandbags and uniforms. This too was war work.

KHAKI MAGIC

Oh! Toil grimly at your weaving
At your belting and your sleeving,
At the cloth you're cutting in that dusty room!
Hear the battle-song enthralling!
For the bugle's clearly calling,
And the boys are wanting khaki from your loom.

They have left the women weeping,
They have left the children sleeping,
They come laughing be it glory, be it doom.
'Tis to make the brave ones braver
'Tis to prove the grave need graver,
That the boys are asking khaki from your loom.

Oh! work wisely at your scheming
At your sewing and your seaming!
'Tis a magic stuff you're weaving in that gloom!
'Tis to make the youngsters older
'Tis to make the weaklings bolder
That the boys are wanting khaki from your loom.

Kathleen Braimbridge

By the middle of 1915, women were needed to do more than supply socks, mufflers, mittens, even uniforms. It was now apparent that the army was woefully short of all types of armaments and, with the growing demand for increasing numbers of men to enlist – initially voluntarily and from early 1916 through conscription – women had to be encouraged to enter the munitions factories.

If women's involvement in munitions work was fundamental to the war effort, for many, it was still controversial, both in terms of the supposedly high wages they were earning (which very broadly ranged from around 30 shillings to £2 a week with deductions for lodgings and meals) and their involvement, albeit at one remove, in the destruction of life. Women were supposed to be the givers of life not its annihilators. Its contentious nature, as well as the excitement and antagonisms of women's factory work, appears in poetry relating to and written by those upon whom, according to a popular poster of the time, 'His Life Depends'.

Several munitions poems tap into the perception among the middle class that these war workers were simply intent on earning high wages and having a good time. Several poets, reflecting fairly widespread views of the time, failed to see, or conveniently overlooked, how many working class women were desperately in need of reasonably well-paid employment, due to high rates of inflation and the often depressed wages that wartime allowances did not keep up with. These women entered the factories in order both to feed themselves and their families and also out of a sense of patriotism – which many people erroneously believed was a preserve of the more educated sections of society.

Munitions workers were uncomfortably aware that their work was dangerous. Nevertheless, they cheerfully accepted that handling noxious materials, the ever-present danger of explosions, the frequently sub-standard equipment they used, as well as factory owners' widespread disregard for what we now would call 'Health and Safety' legislation, were simply hazards of their job and they turned a blind eye the risks that they ran.

MUNITIONS WAGES

Earning high wages?
Yus, Five quid a week.
A woman, too, mind you,
I calls it dim sweet.

Ye'are asking some questions –
But bless yer, here goes:
I spends the whole racket
On good times and clothes.

Me saving? Elijah!
Yer do think I'm mad.
I'm acting the lady,
But – I ain't living bad.

I'm having life's good times.
See 'ere, it's like this:
The 'oof come o' danger,
A touch-and-go bizz.

We're all here today, mate,
Tomorrow – perhaps dead,
If Fate tumbles on us
And blows up our shed.

Afraid! Are yer kidding?
With money to spend!
Years back I wore tatters,
Now – silk stockings, mi friend!

I've bracelets and jewellery,
Rings envied by friends;
A sergeant to swank with,
And something to lend.

I drive out in taxis,
Do theatres in style.
And this is mi verdict –
It is jolly worth while.

Worth while, for tomorrow
If I'm blown to the sky,
I'll have repaid mi wages
In death – and pass by.

Madeline Ida Bedford

The poem's callous tone suggests that Bedford may not have known that many 'munitioneers' were not only contributing their labour, health, and lives to the War but also their hard-earned money. Posters, a popular method of hectoring the public, urged investment in War Bonds and factory supervisors encouraged 'thrift through War Savings Associations or by other means.' Female workers responded; they crowded into post offices to buy war savings certificates and many also subscribed to wartime charities and benevolent funds. One factory superintendent noted that although many of the workers could not afford to eat in the subsidised factory canteens, nevertheless, 'many [girls] invested substantial amounts in War Savings Certificates'.

This anonymous poem from a scrapbook collection of munitions workers' poems (*Munitions Being Some Verse And Sketches From A War Workers Factory*

'Somewhere In England' Aug 1917, held at the Imperial War Museum) provides
an alternative viewpoint.

WAR LOAN

> We're working on munitions to help to win the war,
> Now England needs more money, so has called on us once more;
> Right gladly would we aid her by giving of our own,
> That's why we are so busy putting money in War Loan:
> So that our gallant fighting men can with conviction say,
> 'Our women tried to aid us in every possible way.'

A number of factories published their own papers in which workers' poems
frequently appeared. These provide a contemporary view of how factory
workers saw themselves and their labour. Probably referring to the Battle of
the Somme – although any major attempt to break through enemy lines and
hasten victory was known as a 'Big Push' – one self-styled 'Hayes Munitionette'
has no qualms, and is indeed proud of the part her fellow munitionettes are
playing:

BIG PUSH

> The big push is in progress
> At the battle front in France
> And the girls of Hayes have now
> The opportunity and chance
> To make their high explosives
> And to work at topmost speed
> To fill and pack the Ammunition
> The stuff the dear boys need.
> It's the first time in our lifetime
> Us girls have had the chance
> To help our best boys when at War
> And we'll make Hun murderers dance.

Whilst munitions workers themselves were proud that they were making
'Hun murderers dance', some observers were far from convinced that this was
an appropriate female role. This much anthologised piece makes the poet's
views plain:

WOMEN AT MUNITION MAKING

Their hands should minister unto the flame of life,
Their fingers guide
The rosy teat, swelling with milk,
To the eager mouth of the suckling babe
Or smooth with tenderness,
Softly and soothingly,
The heated brow of the ailing child.
Or stray among the curls
Of the boy or girl, thrilling to mother love.
But now.
Their hands, their fingers
Are coarsened in munitions factories.
Their thoughts, which should fly
Like bees among the sweetest mind flowers,
Gaining nourishment for the thoughts to be,
Are bruised against the law,
'Kill, kill.'
They must take part in defacing and destroying the natural body
Which, certainly during the dispensation
Is the shrine of the spirit.
O God!
Throughout the ages we have seen,
Again and again
Men by Thee created
Cancelling each other.
And we have marvelled at the seeming annihilation
Of Thy work.
But this goes further,
Taints the fountain head,
Mounts the poison to the Creator's very heart.
O God!
Must It anew be sacrificed on earth?

Mary Gabrielle Collins

It was not only the fact of women making munitions that would prove controversial. Inevitably, in wartime some will prosper financially and several poets found the profits made by factory owners and armament kings distasteful. This point was made forcefully by Ethel Talbot Scheffauer:

SPIDERS
(To All Munitions Profiteers)

The lean grey spiders sat in their den
    And they were starved and cold – –
They said – – Let there be strife among men
    That we may gather gold.

The young men at their toil were brothers
    Over all the earth;
The proud eyes of all their mothers
    Praised them with equal worth.

There came a word in the ears of the young men,
    And they believed and heard,
And there was fire in the eyes of the young men
    Because of that word.

Give yourselves to be shattered and broken,
    Said the spiders aloud;
And know your enemy by this token
    Out of the spider-crowd.

He that has in his eyes a flame,
    And in his hands a trust! – –
Him shall ye smite in Heaven's name – –
    And they played with their yellow dust.

And over the world from morn till even
    The young men awoke and heard,
And slew their like by seventy and seven
    Because of the word.

And every one that died of the young men
    Cried with the same voice;
And the spiders at the fall of the young men
    Cried from their dens – – Rejoice – –

And every mother of all the mothers
    Bled from the same heart;

Yet cried to the young men that were brothers,
　　"In God's name depart."

And the spiders sat in their lighted palace
　　And feasted no more a-cold – –
And redly, out of a burning chalice,
　　Gathered their minted gold.

Ethel Talbot Scheffauer

Most women, unconcerned by the controversy surrounding their making deadly weapons, or even who was profiting from their labour, found that munitions work helped them to feel closer to their men at the Front. Helen Dircks lived in Ealing, near to several munitions factories, and may have even worked in one herself. She felt that munitions workers and soldiers were equally trapped in their new lives:

MUNITIONS

We have forgotten the guelder roses,
You and I,
The lilies
And the lilac too;
The sweet scents of Spring
Pass by unnoticed.

My life
Lies in the turning of a lathe
And yours
In the skill to fight –
Two poor cogs in the machinery of war.

And yet
I cannot help but feel
The wonder veil
Upon our meeting eyes
Hold more
Than peace could ever bring.

Helen Dircks

Irrespective of women's motives for entering the factories, industrial and gender relationships were far from harmonious. Poems in *The Bombshell Magazine of the National Projectile Factory at Templeborough Sheffield*, which in 1918 employed about 5,000 women, reflect both gender and hierarchical tensions. They also draw attention to the harshness of factory life and the particular pressures upon women supervisors or forewomen, who were frequently despised by male workers and disrespected by their female subordinates. All are recurring themes in female munitions workers' memoirs.

Parodying Rudyard Kipling's famous 1895 poem 'If – ', this anonymous writer feels that she and her fellow workers now inhabit a very different world:

IF

If you can keep your head when all about you
The bells are whirring and the hammers ring
If when at first the stop and din astound you
You try to learn and understand each thing:
If you can learn and not be tired of learning
The name and use of all the different m's
And know the look and feel of every turning
And see the refuse sorted from the guns.

If you can keep your galleys clean and flowing
Without the loss of temper or of rake
Nor come back full of indignant glowing
When fruitless hunts for Izal take the cake,
If you can urge and not be called a driver
If you can push on work – and get a smile;
If you make each woman be a striver
And feel that what she's doing is worthwhile.

If you can bear to have your tools all taken
Each day, and never stop to curse the thief,
If when your tubs want emptying you're forsaken
By men, who prefer a plate of beef;
If you can get one mind in all your workers
And make them feel that if they persevere
Their shop will be the cleanest – even shirkers
Must know they've got to do their bit or clear;

If you can make your Brushes, Tubs and Trolleys
To serve their turn long after they are done,
And never think about the last turn's follies
Who *must* have scattered orange peels for fun;
If you can keep the Foreman and Machine Girls
At peace with each one of your chosen few
And see that every red band at the bench hurls
Her orange peel far from public view.

If you last the Shift of eight long hours
At night and never turn a hair 'pro tem.,'
You're a success, and – all the mighty powers
Will say you're just the Forewoman for them.

Anonymous

Editor's Note: Izal was very thin toilet paper which looked and felt like tracing paper.

Lady Kathleen Lindsay was closely connected with the managerial side of munitions work. Although her acrostic 'Munitions Alphabet' gives at times an idealised view of munitions work, there is significant information about the different types of work women were involved in.

MUNITIONS ALPHABET

A stands for number eleven Adapters
Their history is written in several chapters.
B is the bomb projected from trenches
And handled in workshops by hefty young wenches.
C is the cartridge case used with a shell
It makes a nice gong or an ashtray as well.
D Detonators of several grains
Are essential in fuses and useful in gaines.
E the exploder Container whose wheeze is
To be as eccentric as ever it pleases.
F is the Fuze which inspectors delight
To release in large numbers by Saturday night.
G is the Gaine without which the fuze
Its bad reputation at Whitehall might lose.
H is the highest Explosive in guns

Which obedient to orders annihilates Huns.
I the Incendiary shell is a terror
Needing more than one proof to eliminate error.
J is for jellite, I shouldn't advise you
To sniff it or else the results might surprise you.
K is the keenness with which the staff seek
To work fifty hours at least in the week.
L is for Lewis whose weapon the Yanks
Refused but which England accepted with thanks.
M in the Ministry labour is joy
While the Staff and their friends don't despise the Savoy.
N is the Nine two which looks very lean
When placed besides twelve or a monster Fifteen.
O Obturator expression absurd,
It's just like the Navy to use such a word.
P is the Primer all polished and round
Without which no cartridge case ought to be found.
Q is Q.F. Ammunition required
By millions and millions so fast it is fired.
R is the absolute certain rejection
Awaiting all items that don't meet perfection.
S is the Shell which gives all the trouble
That properly handled should burst like a bubble.
T is the Tube and with little restriction
Its use and abuse are developed by friction.
U is the uniform just the right shade
For a trim little, neat little, bright little maid.
V is the vent sealing fiend of Percussion
Whose wayward behaviour has caused much discussion.
W is weight which judged by Statistics
Has very important effects on ballistics.
X is unknown, it's the pay of the staff
That is working for nothing on England's behalf.
Y is the youth on the eighth or ninth floor
Who is madly in love with the typist next door.
Z is the zest that these young people bring
To the Service of Ministry, Country and King.

Kathleen Lindsay

Editor's Note: The 'monster' 15 inch shells were heavy and due to their short range were only used for a short time before being replaced with 12 inch and older 9.2 inch shells.

It is well known that a number of more affluent women became volunteer nurses to avenge the death of a loved one. Similar sentiments also drove a number of these women into munitions work. Theodora Corrin's poem, found in a scrapbook, suggests that her munitions work links her with her beloved.

MUNITIONS WORKS
(An Uncensored Letter)

I cannot sleep at night, my lad,
I'm easier waking too,
While you are fighting far away
There's work for wives to do.

And oh! If all the shells were filled
And every job well done,
If men and guns could all be served
Till every trench was won.

If Victory came in sight at last –
With peace an afterthought –
And reckoning could be made in Hell
For all the havoc wrought;

If through the tranquil future years
The night brought sleep to me,
If darkness held no hidden fears
And our child played at your knee;

I wonder– could our fire of love
Burn with a clearer light,
Than it burns with you at the guns, my lad
And with me at the works tonight.

Theodora Corrin

One aspect of women's munitions work that does not appear in their poetry is the number of women who were killed or severely injured in accidents and disasters in factories. There are only two poetic hints of such disasters: one is the line in 'Munitions Wages' about being blown to the sky; two of the ten verses in 'Ten Little Dornock Girls', published in *Dornock Souvenir Magazine 1919*, also hint at calamities while the other eight verses allude more to factory tensions.

> 'Seven little Dornock girls did some N/G mix
> One was overcome with fumes,
> And then there were six.
> …
> Three little Dornock girls went to work quite new
> The Acid fumes did smother one,
> And then there were two.'

Editor's Note: N/G nitro-glycerine a heavy, colourless, oily, explosive liquid used as an active ingredient in the manufacture of explosives.

The precise numbers of fatalities among female munitions workers are shrouded in mystery. As recorded in *Hansard*, in February 1919, John Davison MP for Smethwick asked James Hope MP, Parliamentary and Financial Secretary to the Ministry of Munitions, about the 'number of employees in His Majesty's munitions factories killed, and the number injured since August, 1914, what number of each section were men and what number women.' The Honourable Gentleman confessed that he did not know. A very conservative estimate would suggest that fatalities alone run into the many hundreds and the numbers of those who suffered life-changing injuries, or even Post Traumatic Stress Disorder, following horrific explosions are equally shrouded in mystery.

Conclusion: 'What of Pierrette?'

The Great War is often considered to have been the first Total War. According to the Oxford Dictionary the term 'Home Front' was coined during the conflict and it was here that the majority of women remained. Although they never left the comparative safety of their own shores, their poetry reveals how the War informed every aspect of their lives. From the moment they bade a heartbreaking farewell to their beloved serviceman, either at the station or, as some preferred, in the privacy of their own home, he was constantly in their thoughts.

An intimate way of showing love to one's own or indeed another woman's beloved was to knit. By knitting one could weave love and luck into every stitch. Knitting created a community and it could also keep unbearable thoughts at bay. Yet, knitting was also part of the war effort. Peacetime uniform suppliers simply could not keep up with the armies' insatiable need for socks and battalions of knitters were mobilised. This was unglamorous work but above all essential and knitters knew that without their efforts the sufferings of the men in trenches and in tented hospitals would have been even greater. The thousands of knitting poems bear witness to the value that both the women and the army placed upon their work.

If knitting was quintessentially feminine, so too was placing food on the table. Queuing for food, battles with shopkeepers, railing against governmental edicts and finding ways of supplementing provisions by growing one's own, became an integral part of women's wartime experiences. This part, almost unmentioned in the historiography of the First World War, like every aspect of women's lives, also found its way into verse.

By 1915, ammunition was running dangerously low. A new army of women was needed and a fresh call went out. But this one was more controversial. If knitting and putting food on the table were essentially feminine activities, manufacturing the weapons of destruction seemed to fly in the face of accepted womanly behaviour. To compound the controversy, some even dared to admit that factory work was an improvement on skivvying. Other poets take a more fatalistic attitude. Munitions poems show women's acceptance that life in the factory could be short; like soldiers, factory workers were mere cogs in the machinery of this Great European War for Civilisation. Yet, irrespective of the controversies surrounding women's munitions work, she 'at her lathe', just like 'he at the front', made possible the Allied Victory in 1918.

Munitions poetry, knitting poems and those relating to bidding farewell give an insight into lives irrevocably changed by the fateful shot that rang out in a distant Bosnian town on 28 June 1914.

Chapter 2

The Power of the Cross:
Religion in Women's Poetry

In 1914, the majority of Britons were, at least nominally, Christian: about 30 million citizens considered themselves Anglican, with significant numbers also adhering to Roman Catholic or Non-Conformist Christian doctrines. Widespread attendance at church or Sunday school, hymn-singing in school assemblies, daily prayers and readings from religious texts meant almost everyone had some knowledge of the Bible. The church's annual festivals punctuated the year and biblical references and allusions were widely understood, offering comfort in times of personal and national stress.

For those subscribing to the Anglican doctrine, one of the Thirty-Nine Articles of the Church of England enshrined during the reign of Elizabeth I, confirmed that, despite being founded by the Prince of Peace, 'it is lawful for Christian men at the commandment of the magistrate to wear weapons and serve in the wars.' Although Christ is often referred to as 'The Prince of Peace', military service has been considered a legitimate Christian activity since the fourth century of the Christian Era, when the Roman Emperor Constantine had a vision of the Cross inscribed with the words 'By this symbol you will conquer'.

After the mid-nineteenth century Crimean War, hymns using military language – even if they spoke of a battle between Good and Evil as opposed to armies, had gained in popularity, culminating in 1865 with 'Onward Christian Soldiers' (originally written to be sung by children). Yet, despite these religious undertones, early twentieth century life had become increasingly secularised; amongst the poorer classes, disenchantment with religion had set in and even the ostensibly faithful had relatively little time for religion.

Immediately following the declaration of war, the highest ecclesiastic authorities reassured the faithful that this was a Holy War waged against the forces of evil. In the pre-war years, churchmen had denounced the nation as indolent, oblivious to the teachings of Jesus Christ. Now, through the actions of her sons who would march to war under the banner of the Church Militant, and the selflessness of her daughters, who could show their love and compassion for suffering humanity by offering their services to the Red Cross, national redemption was at hand. Thousands of laypeople and clerics hoped that some form of religious revival would sweep across a newly purified Britain which, by the end of the War, would be a truly Christian land.

The 'religious revival' in women's war poetry

From August 1914, church attendance rose amongst all denominations, with churchgoers seeking both solace and reassurance from religious leaders that the nation's cause was just and God was on their side. Ideas of former indifference and a wartime return to religion are summed up in what became the War's most widely anthologised poem.

CHRIST IN FLANDERS

We had forgotten You, or very nearly —
You did not seem to touch us very nearly—
Of course we thought about You now and then;
Especially in any time of trouble —
We knew that You were good in time of trouble –
But we are very ordinary men.

And there were always other things to think of —
There's lots of things a man has got to think of—
His work, his home, his pleasure, and his wife;
And so we only thought of You on Sunday —
Sometimes, perhaps, not even on a Sunday —
Because there's always lots to fill one's life.

And, all the while, in street or lane or byway
In country lane, in city street, or byway —
You walked among us, and we did not see.
Your feet were bleeding as You walked our pavements —
How *did* we miss Your footprints on our pavements? —
Can there be other folk as blind as we?

Now we remember; over here in Flanders —
(It isn't strange to think of You in Flanders) —
This hideous warfare seems to make things clear.
We never thought about You much in England —

But now that we are far away from England,
We have no doubts, we know that You are here.

You helped us pass the jest along the trenches —
Where, in cold blood, we waited in the trenches —
You touched its ribaldry and made it fine.
You stood beside us in our pain and weakness —
We're glad to think You understand our weakness —
Somehow it seems to help us not to whine.

We think about You kneeling in the Garden —
Ah! God! the agony of that dread Garden —
We know You prayed for us upon the cross.
If anything could make us glad to bear it —
'Twould be the knowledge that You willed to bear it —
Pain — death — the uttermost of human loss.

Though we forgot You — You will not forget us —
We feel so sure that You will not forget us —
But stay with us until this dream is past.
And so we ask for courage, strength, and pardon —
Especially, I think, we ask for pardon —
And that You'll stand beside us to the last.

                                L W [Lucy Whitmell]

Inspired partly by the well-established female tradition of hymn-writing, many women wrote and published poems that either resemble or were composed as hymns. The *Saturday Westminster Gazette* frequently proposed poetry competitions to its readers. One category which attracted many entries requested 'suitable hymnodic poems for this time of conflict'. A number of the entries were highly bellicose. However, the joint winner was:

AN EVENING HYMN IN TIME OF WAR

In this sad-time when war clouds skim our sky,
Sun, moon and stars no light of hope afford;
From out the gloom we raise to Thee our cry,
Lighten our darkness we beseech Thee, Lord.

To all who nobly perish in the fight,
Grant thine eternal peace, their soul's reward,
For those who sacrifice health, limbs or sight,
Lighten their darkness, we beseech Thee Lord.

Protect all helpless victims of the strife,
Comfort the hearts bereaved by fire and sword,
And make us brave in facing death or *Life*
Lighten our darkness we beseech thee Lord.

Mrs Hamilton-Fellowes

From the day hostilities were declared, a number of women had been unashamedly anti-war. Unsurprisingly, overtly pacifist women poets also discovered in Christianity a suitable theme for their despair – and they found publishers willing to publish their work.

WAR BETWEEN CHRISTIANS

The seamless robe of Christ is rent asunder
Once more; the guns His thrice-reiterant prayer
("That they may all be one"*) mock everywhere;
The Cross stands shamed; the very heathen wonder.

Great is our land indeed, our cause yet greater.
But Law, not War, should right the Christian's wrong!
Did we but feign to echo Bethlehem's song.
Or yields the early Gospel to a later?

Is it His own who compass His dethroning?
To that sharp crown of Christ so meekly worn
Add we, called Christians, yet another thorn?
Was then for this, but this, His blood atoning?

O Teuton! hating so thy brother Briton,
O Briton! hating him, unto the death.
Forbear! for ye are both of Nazareth;
For both, Love's law was sealed and signed and written.

A great Light bear we to the lands yet darkened:
Through us, the bearers, shall it flicker and fall
"Of one blood have I made the nations all" —
O Lord! the word is Thine, but who hath hearkened?

[Editor: * *See John xvii. 11, 21 and 22*]

S Gertrude Ford

'She wears no weapon of attack': Nurses and poetry

From the very beginning, nurses, be they professionals or volunteers, saw at first-hand the result of this 'war between Christians'. Some accepted that it was Holy, others vehemently denied this construction. Professional army nurses left for the Front within days of war being declared. Members of the Voluntary Aid Detachments (VAD) and those who held Red Cross Nursing Certificates were quick to offer their services, initially for home duties. A relatively small number eventually served in Base or General Hospitals overseas, although never in Casualty Clearing Stations.

Belief in the nobility and sanctity of nursing service was widespread and reinforced by the religious emblem emblazoned on the aprons of those working under the aegis of the British Red Cross. VAD leaders were keen to remind women of their high calling. On her departure from England, every volunteer was given a copy of a prayer written by Rachel Crowdy, the VAD Commandant in France and Belgium, which overtly connected the Cross borne by Christ with the Red Cross on the volunteers' aprons. Another early VAD leader, Margaret Ampthill, reminded women, 'Every VAD member wears on her uniform a cross which for 1900 years has been the emblem of an ideal life; and you have therefore to uphold that standard.' Though a few were cynical, one going so far as to pen, 'Fat Chance!' in the margin of her copy, many took the admonition to heart.

Yet, the realities of military nursing were more complex than simply living an ideal life. The primary aim of military medical services is to patch a man up so that he can return to active service. American Nurse Margaret Helen Florine RN from San Francisco is one of a very small number of poets who may be questioning this aspect of a nurse's role, asking whether the successful fulfilment of her duty simply meant that a man was given another chance to kill or be killed.

TO A RED CROSS NURSE

You're as great as any hero,
In the bloody strife,
He can give unto his country
    But one sacred life.
You, if faithful to your trust,
Send back to satisfy the lust,
A hundred who, when cause is just
    Will follow drum and fife!
The hundred you return to fight
Have suffered, bled, faced death and when
They *know* that they are in the right
    Are worth two hundred men.

Margaret Helen Florine RN

Perhaps because confronting the part they are playing in returning a man to fight poses uncomfortable questions, most nurses prefer to praise their patients' steadfastness. Although VAD Eva Dobell edges towards questioning the part she and her colleagues are playing, nevertheless she pulls back from pushing the thought to its final, logical conclusion.

PLUCK

Crippled for life at seventeen,
His great eyes seems to question why:
With both legs smashed it might have been
Better in that grim trench to die
Than drag maimed years out helplessly.

A child – so wasted and so white,
He told a lie to get his way,
To march, a man with men, and fight
While other boys are still at play.
A gallant lie your heart will say.

So broke with pain, he shrinks in dread
To see the 'dresser' drawing near;
And winds the clothes about his head

That none may see his heart-sick fear.
His shaking, strangled sobs you hear.

But when the dreaded moment's there
He'll face us all, a soldier yet,
Watch his bared wounds with unmoved air,
(Though tell-tale lashes still are wet),
And smoke his Woodbine cigarette.

Eva Dobell

[Editor: *'Dressings' were the most dreaded part of the day for patients and nursing personnel. In this pre-antibiotics era, in an attempt to avoid gas gangrene, wounds had to be disinfected, often twice daily, with powerful antiseptics such as iodine and carbolic, a frequently agonising procedure which both parties knew would have to be repeated in a few short hours. Often seen as 'nerve-soothers', cigarettes were frequently given to wounded soldiers and smoking in the wards and during dressings was commonplace.*]

The First Geneva Convention of 1864 stated that, regardless of which side he had fought on: 'if a member of the armed forces is wounded or sick, and therefore in no condition to take an active part in the hostilities, he is no longer part of the fighting force and becomes a vulnerable person in need of protection and care.' Furthermore, irrespective of their status, all medical personnel, hospitals and ambulances were neutral. In this poem, found in a *Scrapbook of Poems on the Great European War*, the neutrality of nurses is singled out for praise in pseudo-religious language.

THE RED CROSS NURSE

She is in the foremost battle she is in the rearmost tent,
She wears no weapon of attack no armour of defence,
She is braver than the bravest, she is truer than the true,
She asks not if the soldier struck for red and white and blue,
She asks not if he fell beneath the yellow and the red;
She is mother to the wounded, she is sister to the dead.
The victor's cheers ring in her ears but these she does not heed;
The victim's groans and dying moans are given as her meed,
And many a suffering hero choked his blind and sullen curse,
To smooth it to a blessing for the Red Cross Army Nurse.

Work on, O noble army nurse and the Crown of Crowns be yours,
Not always shall destruction be the glory which endures.
It is coming – it is coming; you are helping on the day,
When we learn the nobler action is to succour not to slay.

Anonymous

The poet idealises nurses' neutrality, perhaps not realising that respecting this could, for some at least, be a struggle and initially many nurses worried about the need to show compassion to those whose countrymen had potentially wounded or killed their own loved ones. VAD Vera Brittain was not alone in confessing to feelings of dread when she heard that she was detailed for duty in a German prisoners' ward. Yet, she soon came to accept that soldiers from the opposing sides shared a common humanity. Like many nurses, Brittain used religious undertones to poeticize her service and her admiration for those working and suffering in the German Prisoners' ward.

THE GERMAN WARD

When the years of strife are over and my recollection fades
 Of the wards wherein I worked the weeks away,
I shall still see, as a vision rising 'mid the War- time shades,
 The ward in France where German wounded lay.

I shall see the pallid faces and the half-suspicious eyes,
 I shall hear the bitter groans and laboured breath,
And recall the loud complaining and the weary tedious cries,
 And the sights and smells of blood and wounds and death.

I shall see the convoy cases, blanket-covered on the floor,
 And watch the heavy stretcher-work begin,
And the gleam of knives and bottles through the open theatre door,
 And the operation patients carried in.

I shall see the Sister standing, with her form of youthful grace,
 And the humour and the wisdom of her smile,
And the tale of three years' warfare on her thin expressive face-
 The weariness of many a toil-filled while.

I shall think of how I worked for her with nerve and heart and mind,
  And marvelled at her courage and her skill,
And how the dying enemy her tenderness would find
  Beneath her scornful energy of will.

And I learnt that human mercy turns alike to friend or foe
  When the darkest hour of all is creeping nigh,
And those who slew our dearest, when their lamps were burning low,
  Found help and pity ere they came to die.

So, though much will be forgotten when the sound of War's alarms
  And the days of death and strife have passed away,
I shall always see the vision of Love working amidst arms
  In the ward wherein the wounded prisoners lay.

Vera Brittain

Nursing personnel were frequently accorded semi–divine status in posters, postcards and also in poetry. The most overt link between women, the Madonna, the soldiers and Jesus Christ occurs in Alonzo Foringer's American Red Cross poster, in which a giant nurse cradles a diminutive soldier on a stretcher. The slogan reads, 'The Greatest Mother in the World'. Nurses were often poeticised in maternal terms, both by patients and by other women, including nurses themselves.

A SISTER IN A MILITARY HOSPITAL

Blue dress, blue tippet, trimmed with red,
White veil, coif-like about her head.
Starched apron, cuffs, and cool, kind hands,
Trained servants to her quick commands.
Swift feet that lag not to obey
In diligent service day by day.

A face that would have brought delight
To some pure-souled pre-Raphaelite;
Madonna of a moment, caught
Unwary in the toils of thought,
Stilled in her tireless energy,
Dark-eyed and hushed with sympathy.

Warm, eager as the south-west wind,
Straight as a larch and gaily kind
As pinewood fires on winter eves,
Wholesome and young as April leaves,
Four seasons blent in rare accord
— You have the Sister of our ward.

Winifred Letts

Prize-winning poet and VAD Alberta Vickridge recognizes nurses' need
to control their emotions in the face of soldiers' sufferings. This need and the
daily agonies they witnessed, took a considerable toll on nursing personnel,
leading to a number suffering mental breakdowns and a few even taking their
own lives. Parenthetically, no poet has written about shell-shocked or PTSD
nurses, although shell-shocked soldiers occasionally appear in women's poems.

Vickridge also sees the maternal connection between nurses and patients.
In their diaries and memoirs, nurses write about occasions when, at the end,
a soldier confused the nurse with his mother and believed that it was she who
was easing him into the next life.

THE RED CROSS SISTER

Indomitable and aloof,
She moves along the sunny ward:
Beneath their folds of spotless woof
        Her brows are calm: her eyes regard
        Like frost, is bright and keen and hard.
No pitying tear must stain her cheek;
She looks on pain emotionless,
For she, to whom the maimed and weak
        Turn daily in their blind distress,
        Must pray for strength and steadfastness.
Austere she seems, aloof, apart,
Yet starred upon her linen's snow,
The Red Cross trembles o'er her heart,
        The scarlet flower of ruth, whose glow
        In secret warms the breast below.
Who knows her thoughts? Since in the deeps
Of every woman's heart, the same
Strong mother-love unchanging sleeps,

> Perchance unchilded, hers would claim
> All children hurt in life's rough game.
> And, secret from ridiculers,
> She holds in tender memory
> These wounded boys, – these babes of hers –
> Some healed and gone and some whose cry
> Has named her in death's agony.

Alberta Vickridge

'Dreadful and horrid death': Christian symbols

In the heightened religious atmosphere of the day and with the Red Cross so highly visible and soldiers' sufferings so agonising, it is unsurprising that the Cross, ideas of redemption through suffering, and Christian symbols found their way into nurses' and civilians' wartime poetry.

Roman Catholic Mary Henderson served with the Scottish Women's Hospital Units for Foreign Service (SWH). The prosaic title of the her poem implies this is just one of many incidents she has witnessed in makeshift hospitals in Serbia, where hundreds of wounded lay on straw pallets on every inch of available space. Like many nursing personnel, she sees the link between the wounded Christ and modern-day soldiers. She may even be daring to suggest that her patients' agonies are greater than His.

AN INCIDENT

> He was just a boy, as I could see,
> For he sat in the tent there close by me.
> I held the lamp with its flickering light,
> And felt the hot tears blur my sight
> As the doctor took the blood-stained bands
> From both his brave, shell-shattered hands--
> His boy hands, wounded more pitifully
> Than Thine O Christ, on Calvary.
>
> I was making tea in the tent where they,
> The wounded, came in their agony;
> And the boy turned when his wounds were dressed,
> Held up his face like a child at the breast,
> Turned and held his tired face up,
> For he could not hold the spoon or cup,

And I fed him ... Mary, Mother of God,
All women tread where thy feet have trod.

And still on the battlefield of pain
Christ is stretched on His Cross again;
And the Son of God in agony hangs,
Womanhood striving to ease His pangs.
For each son of man is a son divine,
Not just to the mother who calls him 'mine',
As he stretches out his stricken hand,
Wounded to death for the Mother Land.

Mary Henderson

Henderson seems to accept or at least be resigned to soldiers' sufferings; not so Mary Borden, who in a long, modernist poem points an accusatory finger at those who send unidentified soldiers to an agonising death, disguising it as their Christian duty. The conditions for French *poilus* with whom Borden worked were significantly worse than for British and Imperial forces. Many truly were cattle fodder.

UNIDENTIFIED

Look well at this man. Look!
Come up out of your graves, philosophers,
And you who founded churches, and all you
Who for ten thousand years have talked of
God...
For you have something interesting to learn
By looking at this man.

Stand all about, you many-legioned ghosts,
Fill up the desert with your shadowy forms,
And in the vast resounding waste of death,
Watch him while he dies;
He will not notice you...

He waits for death;
He watches it approach;
His little bloodshot eyes can see it bearing

down on every side;
He feels it coming underneath his feet, running, burrowing underneath the
    ground;
He hears it screaming in the frantic air.
Death that tears the shrieking sky in two,
That suddenly explodes out of the festering
bowels of the earth...

You scorned this man.
He was for you an ordinary man.
Some of you pitied him, prayed over his
soul, worried him with stories of Heaven
and Hell.
Promised him Heaven if he would be
ashamed of being what he was,
And everlasting sorrow if he died as he had
lived, an ordinary man...
None of you trusted him.
No one of you was his friend...

Go back, poor ghosts. Go back into your
graves.
He has no use for you, this nameless man.
Scholars, philosophers, men of God, leave
this man alone.
No lamp you lit will show his soul the way;
No name restore his lost identity.
The guns will chant his death march down
the world.
The flare of cannon light his dying;
The mute and nameless men beneath his
feet will welcome him beside them in the
mud.
Take one last look and leave him standing
there,
Unfriended, unrewarded, and unknown.

Mary Borden

If relatively few poets had personal experience of soldiers' Front Line sufferings, women were intimately aware of mothers' emotional agony. A striking feature of women's religious poetry is the ease with which predominantly Protestant women portrayed themselves/were portrayed as a Mater Dolorosa, with significant numbers turning to Mary, believing that She, above all women, understood their pain.

One unidentified poet, calling her collection simply *Poems of a Mother*, is amongst the many female poets to speak directly of this relationship.

TO OUR LADY OF SORROWS

Mother, you knew beneath the Cross
More than a mother's pain and loss;
Our sons have suffered too and died,
And so our place is at your side,
Watching with you the Crucified.

You gave him freely up to die,
But O you know the agony!
Show us poor others how you bore
To watch His passion slow and sore
Until the end came and He died.

O Mother take us home with you;
Your home was sad and empty too
For three long days – sweet John was there,
But all your grief he could not share,
O Mother of the Crucified.

No son is like the sons that gave
Their lives the suffering to save;
O Mother, let us wait and hold
The comfort of your garment's fold,
And watch your grief and holy pride.

'A Mother'

A member of a Non-Conformist (Christian) sect, Mrs Stephen Parker sums up the comfort many non-Catholic women gained, much to their bemusement, in turning to Mary.

THE CONVERT

When I had my son in the house about me, or working there at the bench
    in the shed,
I hadn't a care in the world to fret me – and now it's a year since my son's
    dead.
Dead and buried he is in Flanders, in a nameless grave I shall never see,
I shall go to him – (God send it early!) – but he will never return to me.

They came to me with their oil of comfort – tender women and men of
    God,
Bidding me think with pride and joy of that poor grave under the blood-
    drenched sod.
Flowers and holy books they brought me, prayed, whispered and went
    away –
And my breast was locked on my grief like a prison: I dreaded the night
    and I hated the day.

I think I had come to the brink of madness, the sun was darkened the
    moon was gone:
It seemed God had made a wheel for his pleasure, to see me bound and
    broken upon.
I had thought so long on my son and his dying, there in the dark in his
    ebbing blood,
When there came a thought of our Lord's Dear Mother – They took her
    son. She understood.

I can't say I'm truly a Catholic, can I? I was a Methodist born and bred!
I never could hold with confessing to priests, and I trouble no one to pray
    for my dead.
But when my grief is a pall about me, and my tortured heart knows no release,
I tell it all to our Lord's Dear Mother - She understands and She gives
    me peace.

Mrs Stephen Parker

In Roman Catholic France, statues of Mary were ubiquitous. The 'Leaning
Virgin of Albert' became the most famous example during the First World
War. Working a mere five miles from the small town of Albert, Mary Borden
would have known that in January 1915, the golden statue of the Virgin atop
the town's impressive Basilica had been shelled. However, despite hanging at a

precarious angle, she did not fall to the ground. A legend developed that victory within the year would go to whichever side succeeded in toppling her. To many serving personnel the very fact that she had not fallen proved that God was determined to protect the Virgin and redemption would come through Her to suffering humanity.

Borden's view is bleaker, however. In her poem even the Holy Mother is powerless to save Herself, Her Child or humankind.

THE VIRGIN OF ALBERT

Oh, the poor Virgin!
She is throwing herself from Heaven;
She is plunging down from the high tower with the child in her hands.
Look, hold your breath, watch the awful gesture of her divine despair
Her golden figure shoots head downwards through the air
The red carcase of the Church gapes beneath her
The ragged skeleton of the tower holds her up
High above the ruined town.
But she is plunging.
With her arms outstretched beyond her head, downward,
With the child in her terrible pointing hands,
She is diving down;
She will dash the child down, on to the stones of the desolate abandoned street.
She has been betrayed.
God has betrayed her.
Oh, the pity!
Oh, the terrible, desperate creature!
She believed in God,
And her people worshipped her,
And because she was the Mother of Compassion,
She stood between them and the anger of God.
For she believed in the love of God.
Lifted up above the city,
Above the little dark homes of her helpless people,
She stood, holding up her child to God.
So for centuries she stood lifted up in her humility and love;
And because God had chosen her and given her a child,
Because she had borne a son to Him,
She believed he would be kind to her people.

One day destruction came like roaring dragons out of Heaven, and fell upon
the town.
Out of the soft mysterious distance invisible monsters came shrieking past
her head.
Flocks of them, unseen, with whistling wings, thick as vultures to a carcase
in a desert,
They swooped down and sprang upon the city.
And the city writhed in their clutches.
Houses staggered, the streets cracked open.
Meek, motionless, holding her child up to Heaven, the Virgin watched from
her tower.
She watched the houses vomit,
Watched them reel like drunkards–fall;
Watched the people running, pouring through the quaking streets with their
treasures piled on wagons;
Watched the wagons smothered, buried, with the horses, the beds and bedding,
the fowls and pretty birds in cages.
She could hear the women and the children screaming;
And the squealing of horses and groaning of cattle and squeaking of pigs caught
in burning stables, sheds, yards.
Helpless, high above them, prisoner in the thundering sky,
Bound to her shaking pedestal, with the church walls giving way beneath her,
She stood holding her child up to God, while her people screamed to her to
save them.
Now the city is deserted.
The people are gone.
The roofless houses and the broken buildings grimace at the Virgin.
The houses of the people who once worshipped her are open filthy places.
The church yawns horrid.
Where the altar was is a heap of dust.
The uncovered apse is choked with debris and the wind and the rain play new
havoc there every day.

Oh the poor desolate Virgin!
She has been abandoned;
She has been betrayed.
God has betrayed her.
She is throwing herself down from Heaven with the child in her terrible
pointing hands.
She is diving down

But she is held.
In the very act of determined despair she is held.
Something holds her suspended in anguish.
Shooting head downwards, she hangs there.
The supreme moment of her unbearable agony is fixed there forever, against
    the sky.
Oh, the poor Virgin!

Mary Borden

Ancient statues and modern-day Christs

A number of soldiers noted in letters and diaries how in Catholic France and
Belgium, Calvaries, symbols of Christ's Passion, dotted the landscape. For the
many thousands of personnel who had never left their native shores, this was
a very visible reminder that they were 'abroad'.

In direct contrast to the loving care with which they had previously been
maintained, during the War these images often became grotesque, disfigured
by bombs, shells and shrapnel. They became part of the physically and
metaphorically shattered landscape and for some poets they symbolized the
destruction, horror and devastation of the War.

Amongst the bleakest of the poems depicting this process is Martha Foote
Crow's, first published in *New York Evening Post* and reprinted in in April
1916 in the (anti-war leaning) *The Nation*.

THE WOODEN CHRIST

At the high ridge
Of a wide war-stricken realm
There stands an ancient wooden Christ.
Hollow the tottering image towers,
Eyeless and rotten, and decrepit there,
His smile a cruel twist.
Within the empty heart of this old Christ
Small stinging insects build their nests;
And iron-hearted soldiers cross themselves
The while they pass
The hollow-hearted figure by.
I think there is no Christ left there
In all those carnage-loving lands
Save only this of hollow wood

With wasps nests
Living in its heart.

Martha Foote Crow

Elinor Jenkins also felt that the statues and images of Christ were reminders of His powerlessness. Both the ancient Christ's and modern-day soldiers' sacrifices appear 'fruitless', pointless in her poem.

ECCE HOMO!

He hung upon a wayside Calvary,
            From whence no more the carven Christ looks down
            With wide, blank eyes beneath the thorny crown,
On the devout and careless, passing by.
The Cross hath shaken with his agony,
            His blood had stained the dancing grasses brown,
            But when we found him, though the weary frown,
That waited on death's long delayed mercy,
Still bent his brow, yet he was dead and cold,
            With drooping head and patient eyes astare,
That would not shut. As we stood turned to ice
The sun remembered Golgotha of old,
            And made a halo of his yellow hair
In mockery of that fruitless sacrifice.

Elinor Jenkins

[Editor: *Pontius Pilate used the words* 'Ecce Homo!' *(Behold the Man), when he presented Christ to the crowd shortly before the Crucifixion – a scene frequently depicted in Christian Art.*]

Muriel Stuart also uses the symbols of the Crucifixion, this time to point out the bleakness of humankind's sacrifice, for strangers.

FORGOTTEN DEAD, I SALUTE YOU

Dawn has flashed up the startled skies,
Night has gone out beneath the hill
Many sweet times; before our eyes
Dawn makes and unmakes about us still

The magic that we call the rose.
The gentle history of the rain
Has been unfolded, traced and lost
By the sharp finger-tips of frost;
Birds in the hawthorn build again;
The hare makes soft her secret house;
The wind at tourney comes and goes,
Spurring the green, harnessed boughs;
The moon has waxed fierce and waned dim:
He knew the beauty of all those
Last year, and who remembers him?

Love sometimes walks the waters still,
Laughter throws back her radiant head;
Utterly beauty is not gone,
And wonder is not wholly dead.
The starry, mortal world rolls on;
Between sweet sounds and silences,
With new, strange wines her breakers brim:
He lost his heritage with these
Last year, and who remembers him?
None remember him: he lies
In earth of some strange-sounding place,
Nameless beneath the nameless skies,
The wind his only chant, the rain
The only tears upon his face;
Far and forgotten utterly
By living man. Yet such as he
Have made it possible and sure
For other lives to have, to be;
For men to sleep content, secure.
Lip touches lip and eyes meet eyes
Because his heart beats not again:
His rotting, fruitless body lies
That sons may grow from other men.

He gave, as Christ, the life he had–
The only life desired or known;
The great, sad sacrifice was made
For strangers; this forgotten dead

Went out into the night alone.
There was his body broken for you,
There was his blood divinely shed
That in the earth lie lost and dim.
Eat, drink, and often as you do,
For whom he died, remember him.

Muriel Stuart

For Christians of all denominations, the service of Holy Communion is the most overt reminder of Christ's sacrifice. The bread and wine are linked to His Body and Blood and the faithful 'eat and drink' in remembrance of Him. These symbols often occur in women's poetry, nowhere more powerfully or more despairingly than in this example by Margaret Sackville.

SACRAMENT

Before the Altar of the world in flower,
Upon whose steps thy creatures kneel in line,
We do beseech Thee in this wild Spring hour,
Grant us, O Lord, thy wine. But not this wine.

Helpless, we, praying by Thy shimmering seas,
Beside Thy fields, whence all the world is fed,
Thy little children clinging about Thy knees,
Cry: 'Grant us, Lord, Thy bread!' But not this bread.

This wine of awful sacrifice outpoured;
This bread of life — of human lives. The Press
Is overflowing, the Wine-Press of the Lord!
Yet doth he tread the foamings no less.

These stricken lands! The green time of the year
Has found them wasted by a purple flood,
Sodden and wasted everywhere, everywhere; —
Not all our tears may cleanse them from that blood.

The earth is all too narrow for our dead,
So many and each a child of ours – and Thine

This flesh (our flesh) crumbled away like bread,
This blood (our blood) poured out like wine, like wine.

Margaret Sackville

Far from providing comfort through associations with Holy Communion and Christ's sacrifice, Vivien Ford is one of a number of poets who felt that such constructions offend the Lord, along with the suggestion that this was a Holy War. She provides a powerful indictment of those who misappropriate Christian liturgy.

THE WORLD'S CHALICE

As if in His still sanctuary He heard
The distant rolling drum,
Upon His carven crucifix the dumb
Stone Jesus stirred.

Stirred, with the everlasting arms out flung
To heal a stricken world,
And wondering, heard the battle challenge hurled
From every tongue.

Then He whose tender side was pierced and torn
On newer wounds looked down,
And saw vast herds in conflict for a crown
That was not thorn.

He for Whom Simon Peter drew the sword
And bidden, put it up,
Beheld again the precious blood outpoured
Into His cup.

'This do' – into His eyes a horror crept –
'In Memory of Me.'
And, as of old in far-off Bethany,
Christ Jesus wept.

Vivien Ford

Conclusion: 'Nearer my God to Thee'

Women who used religion in their war poetry shared a similar background, intimately familiar with the teachings and stories of Christianity. However, the commonality of these tropes and themes does not mean that the women deliver the same messages. One woman's gateway to Heaven is for another a Via Dolorosa; what for one nurse is a sacred service for another is complicity in a house of agony.

Religion helped some women to believe that this was a Holy War. They acknowledged that whatever its cost in human suffering and grief, it would cleanse the nation, and would return apostates to the Christian fold. The outpouring of her sons' sacrificial blood would allow Britannia to rise again, newborn and purified. For 'mothers' who sought to understand the roles that gender forced upon them and their 'sons', religion and especially comparisons with the Holy Family provided a frame of reference.

Irrespective of whether they privileged Her maternity or Her sanctity, women took comfort from knowing that Mary had trodden this very path. Her sufferings gave them strength. By comparing their own and their generation's experience to the Christian story, many poets believed they and their formerly godless nation were moving in the words of the nineteenth century hymn, 'Nearer my God to Thee'.

Other poets, be they nurses or civilians, found little succour in Christianity; they used religious discourse and images to question, even deny their faith. For them, this 'Unholy' War was waged not by new crusaders but by brutalised 'ordinary men' for whom Christianity had become and would remain meaningless. Rather than precious and cleansing, blood was merely effluvia, spilled pointlessly and with profligacy. By their sufferings in the trenches, young men would not rise to eternal life but would rot forever in the Flanders clay.

Just like the hapless 'Virgin of Albert', their mothers, sweethearts, wives had been, 'abandoned', 'betrayed'. The New Testament God of Love did not exist, He was quite simply the Old Testament God of Wrath.

Far from comforting and consoling, Christianity frequently failed to offer solace for a world in which thousands of young men had gone forever. Unable to staunch the blood that Christians were spilling in this so-called Holy War, in Vivien Ford's words even 'Christ Jesus wept'.

Chapter Three

'Lay Your Head on the Earth's Breast': Nature in Women's War Poetry

Poems about the English countryside, generally extolling its beauty, occasionally expressing despair at increasing industrialisation or creeping urbanism, date back to medieval times. The Education Acts of the late nineteenth century had led to an increasingly literate society – and much literacy was taught through poetry, ideally poetry that reinforced a sense of nationalism.

In the early twentieth century, this type of poetry, often referred to as 'Georgian', had become so popular that many soldiers popped anthologies featuring 'nature poetry' into their kit bags before they went overseas. In 1917, the YMCA went so far as to commission an anthology with the telling title, *The Old Country: A Book of Love and Praise of England,* in the hope that poems, prose texts and pictures of thatched cottages with roses round the door, would, in the words of the editor Ernest Rhys, 'hearten home-sick men'. The service-green volume was designed to be the ideal size for a soldier's knapsack.

Little matter that the majority of soldiers hailed from the urban sprawls and slums of industrialised England, the Old Country was assumed to exist in their imaginations and their hearts. This point was not missed by Leicestershire vicar's wife Emily Orr.

A RECRUIT FROM THE SLUMS

'What has your country done for you,
Child of a city slum,
That you should answer her ringing call
To man the gap and keep the wall
And hold the field though a thousand fall
And help be slow to come?

"What has your country given to you,
Her poor relation and friend?
'Oh, a fight like death for your board and keep,

And some pitiful silver coins per week
And the thought of the 'house' at the end.

'What can your country ask from you,
Dregs of the British race?'
'She gave us little, she taught us less,
And why we were born we could hardly guess
Till we felt the surge of the battle press
And looked the foe in the face.'

'Greater love hath no man than this
That a man should die for his friend.'
'We thought life cruel, and England cold;
But our bones were made from the English mould,
And when all is said, she's our mother old
And we creep to her breast at the end.'

Emily Orr

[Editor: *The 'house' is the dreaded workhouse, where many of England's poor feared ending their days.*]

A 'Misty Sea-Girt Island': Visions of home

Although the pieces selected for *The Old Country* were invariably positive and uplifting, throughout the War both male and female poets used the beauty of their native land as a vehicle to express their thoughts about the conflict. Rural poetry lent itself to pain and anguish, as well as patriotism and the affirmation that the War was a just one and God was on the Allies' side.

On 10 October 1914, Alice Meynell became the first woman to have a war poem published in *The Times*. She, like so many poets who used nature to deliver their message, contrasted the last long hot summer of the peace with events unfolding across the Channel:

SUMMER IN ENGLAND 1914

On London fell a clearer light;
    Caressing pencils of the sun
Defined the distances, the white
    Houses transfigured one by one,

The "long, unlovely street" impearled.
    O what a sky has walked the world!

Most happy year! And out of town
    The hay was prosperous, and the wheat;
The silken harvest climbed the down;
    Moon after moon was heavenly sweet,
Stroking the bread within the sheaves,
    Looking twixt apples and their leaves.

And while this rose made round her cup,
    The armies died convulsed; and when
This chaste young silver sun went up
    Softly, a thousand shattered men,
One wet corruption, heaped the plain,
    After a league-long throb of pain.

Flower following tender flower, and birds,
    And berries; and benignant skies
Made thrive the serried flocks and herds.
    Yonder are men shot through the eyes,
    And children crushed. Love, hide thy face
From man's unpardonable race.

A Reply

Who said "No man hath greater love than this
    To die to serve his friend?"
So these have loved us all unto the end.
    Chide thou no more, O thou unsacrificed!
The soldier dying dies upon a kiss,
    The very kiss of Christ.

Alice Meynell

The final stanza, printed either as an ellipsis or with the words 'A Reply',
suggests Meynell found her own vision intolerable, she orders non-combatants,
the 'unsacrificed', to accept the soldiers' sacrifice – and their own passive roles.
Sacrifice for the preservation of England is a recurring theme in nature poetry;
some poets see it as worthwhile whilst others question, sometimes cryptically,

whether any ideal warrants the spilling of so much blood. This tension is a constant feature of women's more sophisticated pastoral poems.

Whilst some of Meynell's imagined 'thousand shattered men' would have been killed, others would have been more or less seriously wounded, the majority clinging to the hope of a 'Blighty ticket' sending them home for hospital treatment. Staff Nurse Beatrice Hopkinson, a member of the Territorial Forces Nursing Service, is among the many nurses who wrote of how patients who had lost a limb or suffered serious injury would remark that they had got 'a nice Blighty one'.

Many nurses and volunteers working in hospitals overseas frequently comment on their patients' overwhelming desire to see England again. This may lie behind Sheffield poet Constance Ada Renshaw's 'The Lure of England'. Superficially, the poem might seem to be a maudlin attempt to sanitize the soldier's sufferings using popular pastoral tropes; a closer reading both of the poem and even the word 'Lure', reveals layers of meaning. Renshaw may be implying that the 'boys' have been duped into sacrificing their sight, their health, their lives.

The 'broken thing' has been emasculated and permanently dislocated by war. All that is left to him is the possibility that he can be returned to and healed by the idealized country he bled for.

THE LURE OF ENGLAND

There's a misty sea-girt island in the sunset-haunted west;
    I can see it in my wounded dreams of home.
I can see the dwindling hedgerows where the sparrow builds her nest,
    And the grass-land with its throw of daisied foam.

Oh! there's Spring upon the island, and the greening lures me back
    To mysterious meres and woodways in the west.
They have stripped my manhood from me, they have stretched me on the rack,
    Take me home, a blinded broken thing, to rest!

I can never see the island with its fields of sheeted gold,
    And the wisps of sunset drifting in the west.
Darkness drowns the dim green valleys and the silent hills of old,
    And the hedges where the sparrow builds her nest.

Let me put my blind eyes down among the bluebells and the grass.
    Let me feel the brimming coolness on my brow.

Let me touch the dewy bracken where the dreamful shadows pass.
    I have bled for England! . . . Let her heal me now!

England, misty England, grey and vague across the sea!
    All your blue-bells bloom in May-time, and your skies are throbbing blue,
Here, the streams are streaked with crimson, and red Death is haunting me.
    — England, England! all my hungry heart is yearning back to you !

My misty sea-girt island in the sunset-laden west!
    I can feel your moorland wind upon my eyes;
I can hear your sleepy birdeens in their swaying moonlit nest . . .
    England — England! . . . with your bluebells and your skies !

Constance Ada Renshaw

Renshaw is far from alone in imagining that thoughts of their native land provide soldiers with comfort. British-born Australian-resident Margery Ruth Betts imagined Australian soldiers also dreaming of their distant homeland.

DEAD MEN'S DREAMS

Strong as the wings of sea-gulls in their flying,
    Glad as the feet that tread the homeward track,
So do their dreams wing home when they are dying.
    Daylong and nightlong, so do they come back.

Like to the incense in the hallowed places,
    All hushed and dim and sweet with faith and prayer,
So do their thoughts, above the purple spaces,
    Hover — a fragrance in the sunlit air.

Above the clang of guns and bugles singing,
    There sang your voice, on distant southern sea,
In dying ears a cry of victory ringing,
    And, hearing, they were conquerors, and free.

Dear cliffs, by winds and ocean-surges riven.
    Dear sand-dunes, high upheld to star and sun,
They dreamt of you, and you were far as Heaven,
    And dear as home, when day and work are done.

You southern sea, and stormy, wind-swept beaches.
And sand-dunes sunkissed in the sunlit air,
And distant ridge and purple moorland reaches,
It is with dead men's dreams that you are fair!

Margery Ruth Betts

Public parks and Zeppelin raids

Despite the proliferation of poetry about an idealized home country, for the majority of British citizens, the rural idyll did not extend beyond an urban park. These had flourished during the Victorian era – civic dignitaries had hoped that parks would re-connect an increasingly brutalized working population with their rustic roots.

During the War, women poets used these public spaces to develop the contrast between the safety of the homeland and the horrors unfolding 'over there'. Edith Mary Cruttwell is one of a number of poets to see the contrast between parks in paradisiacal England, where people can stroll at their will, and the horrors of the Front.

SUNDAY EVENING IN A PUBLIC PARK

The people wander to and fro,
The scarlet tulips nod and glow;
The church-bells drown the shrilling train
And laughter heard and lost again.
. . . .

It is a pretty patch-work sight,
And who can look and not delight?
This Paradise remains the same
Though Europe writhe in hot hell-flame;
And still the scarlet tulips glow,
The people wander to and fro.

Edith Mary Cruttwell

By the summer of 1915, the German High Command had decided that a possible way to break down British resistance and morale and secure victory was to use Zeppelins and aerial attacks on the civilian population. For about fifteen months there was a belief that dirigible airships could break England's insular security through conducting raids over London and other cities. A significant attack was planned over London for 9 August and, although this and the subsequent one on 12 August was unsuccessful, a further attack on 7 September resulted in eighteen fatalities and thirty-eight people injured.

In terms of total casualties of the War, these numbers of lives lost are infinitesimal, but the shock to civilians was enormous. Now death could rain down from the skies on the most innocent civilians – six children were killed during this attack. Viviane Verne's peaceful daytime visit to the quintessentially English Kensington Gardens in London, reminded her how even the night-time sky was being violated by Zeppelin attacks.

KENSINGTON GARDENS (1915)

Dappling shadows on the summer grass,
Vernal rivalry among the trees;
Lovers smiling coyly as they pass,
Sparrows laughing in the summer breeze.

Children playing by the placid lake,
Coaxing ducks, with greedy eyes;
Sunlight gilding riplets that break
Where they struggle for a prize.

Jealous dogs that 'do delight'
In frantic grappling for a stick,
Racing back with 'bark and bite'.
To yield a trophy quite historic.

Lonely ladies dreaming in bath–chairs,
Old men taking sun baths on their seats,
Nurses softly talking in prim pairs,
Telling of their soldier lovers' feats.

Medall'd patrols keeping austere guard,
Over radiant rose and ever-greens,
Gold-flecked finery and velvet sward,
And the quiet garden of dead queens.

Fleecy cloud in limpid blue,
Smiling down with tender mien;
Life seems simple, honest, true,
In this simple open scene.

Who would think that vault benign
God's last area free from vice,
Initiates the aerial mine,
With babes below as sacrifice.

Sitting here on summer morn,
With the birds and babes at play.
Who could dream that sky was torn
Yesternight – with hellish spray

It is strange that Nature's lurement
Waits – unclaimed – for our retrievement,
While men war in false endurement
Deeming this life's great achievement.

Viviane Verne

During her November 1915 visit to London, American nurse Helen Mackay
poeticizes the contrast between the urban park and the encroaching outside
world where searchlights sweep the sky for Zeppelins.

PARK

Beyond the dim wide, mysterious spaces of the park,
the great somber trees and the gleaming water
and the few, pale-gold lamps –
that were not round moons any more, but delicate half-moons –
beyond the haunting of it,
there were roofs and chimneys,
dark in the darkening sky.
And there was a dimmed, darkened abiding of lights in windows,
and a dimmed, darkened travel of lights in the streets,
up and down.

There were great wide marvellous streamers of white light,
shafts of white light,
that swept the city over and over.
Because, beyond all these things there was war.

Helen Mackay

The psychological effects and the fear that the attacks engendered were considerable. For the first time since April 1746 and the Battle of Culloden, war was being waged on British soil. Yet it was not being waged against professional soldiers but against civilians; women and children on the Home Front were the victims. To make matters worse, as the War progressed, the German hit-rate increased. Civilian deaths, and in particular children's deaths, were seen as particularly outrageous.

The Home and War Fronts were merging and although soldiers were fighting overseas to keep England safe, they were only partially successful as their own families were targets. Nonetheless, displaying admirable stoicism, mothers and children picked up the pieces of their lives.

FORTITUDE

Today down Blank Court East, the children shout,
And calm faced women hang their washing out.
　　Ten days ago a bomb fell in the Court
And wiped the smile from out a baby's eyes:
It wrecked the home of Simpkins who had fought
And still is fighting under foreign skies:
　　And blinded little Billy as he brought
For Mother's praise his precious drawing prize.
　　Today down Blank Court East, the children shout,
And calm faced women hang their washing out.

Paula Hudd

'Hell's Let Loose': Gardens as sanctuaries

If many soldiers went to the Front accompanied by *The Old Country* with its depictions of thatched cottages and rose gardens, those at home also found that gardens could remind them both of what the soldiers were fighting for and what was being lost. In a selection of sonnets entitled *Ad Mortuum*, a very typically English garden at first comforts and then, with chilling finality, reminds Winifred Letts of all that is being lost.

HEART'S DESIRE

My heart's desire was like a garden seen
On sudden through the opening of a door
In the grey street of life, unguessed before

But now how magic in sun-smitten green:
Wide cedar-shaded lawns, the glow and sheen
Of borders decked with all a gardener's lore,
Long shaven hedges of old yew, hung o'er
With gossamer, wide paths to please a queen,
Whose happy silken skirts would brush the dew
From peonies and lupins white and blue.
Enchanted there I lingered for a space,
Forgetful of the street, of tasks to do.
But when I would have entered that sweet place
The wind rose and the door slammed in my face.

Winifred Letts

The most unusual selection of wartime garden poems occurs in *My Lady's Garden* which, according to its preface, was 'originally planted [in June 1918] to give pleasure to all who have suffered or are suffering, through the War' and to serve as a living tribute and memorial not only to the dead but also to the wounded. Each combatant nation, corps and Service has its own poetic garden or, occasionally, patch of scrub ground in this horticultural tour de force. On a first reading, the poems appear full of hyperbolic language, however, there are hints this is intentional, even ironical, serving to increase awareness of the realities of war, and of its aftermath. Even today's soldiers may be amused by the idea that staff officers are 'red hot pokers and' and at another point in the text their wives are referred to as 'peonies'!

from MY LADY'S GARDEN

There's a wondrous garden, lovingly designed,
For the flowers immortal in our mem'ry grown:
The resplendent heroes – Armies we have known –
Radiant and joyous, fill my Lady's mind
With the Spring and Summer of a glory Garden.

There are shady alleys 'neath the *Maple Tree,
There's a corner glowing with the *Rising Sun,
And a Glade of Laurels made of vict'ries won
By heroic armies, just across the sea,
Glory is the fragrance of my Lady's Garden.

Rhododendrons purple, crimson ramblers glowing,
Spread the joy of colour in a vivid hue;
Pergolas and arbours gather diamond dew
From the iridescence of the river flowing
As a jewelled girdle round my Lady's Garden.

Just beyond its limits, in a scarlet blaze,
Gorgeous red–hot pokers lift their lofty heads
High above the glory of the lesser reds.
First in rank and splendour, dazzling to our gaze,
Are refulgent generals of our glory Garden.

Not within its precincts does their greatness shine,
But they flame as beacons to the wonder War,
In whose light we gather from each Army Corps
Glory, youth and valour for our mem'ry shrine:
The immortal fragrance of my Lady's Garden.

Hackleplume

[Editor: * *The Maple Leaf and Rising Sun represent the Canadian and Australian
troops; the 'lesser reds' are junior Staff Officers.*]

Most garden poems are based either literally or figuratively on those in
England. However, CALT's 'May 1915', published in *The Englishwoman*, shows
that she is deeply aware of the contrast between the relative safety of England
and what is happening on the Western Front.

MAY 1915

Spring's in my garden!
Spring – and the glad rush of life's resurrection triumphant,
Bidding all nature awake to the joy of renewal:
Tossing the fruit-boughs to foam of delicate blossom:
Spreading her carpet of flow'rs for the feet of the children.
Fragrant and dewy, the lilac breathes joy with its perfume –
Rapture's outpoured in the sweet choirs of birds at the dawning.
Borders are blazing with splendour – the scarlet of tulips,
And wallflowers, a glory of gold in the sun – while the chestnut
Lifts up her white candelabra in silent thanksgiving.
Heav'ns' in my garden!

But Hell's let loose in the gardens of France and Flanders!
War, grim and terrible, red-eyed, red-handed stalks naked –
Followed by all his dread offspring of ruin and famine,
Madness of battle and slaughter, and ruthless destruction,
Merciless cruelty and foulness of devils incarnate,
And brood of a myriad horrors, unspeakable, nameless,
Nature turns faint at the thunderous crash of the conflict:
Birds fly affrighted away from the roar of the tumult:
Tender spring blossoms are drenched in the blood of the dying,
Hell's over yonder.

CALT

When this poem was published, the civilian population in England had no experience of the 'roar' of the guns. A year later, these were increasingly audible throughout parts of Southern England, providing a theme for more than one poet, including famous novelist, Rose Macaulay, whose much anthologized poem 'Picnic' depicts a picnic in Surrey in July 1917. On this occasion, the 'guarding walls' the picnickers had built around themselves began to crumble as the sound of the guns interrupted their reverie and reminded them of all that was being sacrificed across the Channel.

In October 1914, Alys Trotter's 20-year-old son Lieutenant Nigel Trotter was killed near Béthune. Like many mothers she commemorated his short life in verse. Here she remembers the happy pre-war times he and his friends had spent in their Sussex garden. By 1917, the sound of the guns penetrates the security of this idyllic spot and reminds her that a similar destiny and grief to her own awaits countless other mothers and sons.

SUMMER, 1917

The garden that I love has roses red.
Crimson and pink the border hedge is bent
With blossom. I remember how you went
With your two schoolboy friends (because we said
We must have good grey paven paths instead
Of gravel), on a day like this, intent
On time's dead handiwork in stones; and leant
Them up against the wall, and laughed. Now dead
And passed is all that laughter, though there bloom
Flowers as ever, sunburnt and sunlit.

And, borne along the wind a hollow boom
Burdens the scented stillness where we sit,
Canon that sound afar. And someone's doom
Is registered as we are hearing it.

Alys Fane Trotter

Across the county border in Kent, a much younger poet, Enid Bagnold, could also hear the guns. Their sinister sound permeates the garden and her life. She knows that the War is robbing her generation of their young adulthood and too many of them were becoming old before their time.

THE GUNS OF KENT

Though I live as is meant
    Very near, very near,
Happiness, joy and content,
And things as they were.

Yet you see what it is:
When you talk of your Dead
I can't sleep in bed!

I am not languid or tired
But young and I wear
Pretty clothes, pretty hats and a band
At night in my hair.

I think as an old woman thinks
That life isn't much,
That on each of my pleasures is writ
Mustn't touch. Mustn't touch.

And my eyes from the star
I withdraw, and my face from the flowers,
This isn't my hour. I withdraw
My life out of this hour.

For there comes very faint, very far,
    As such voices are

A sound I can hear. That I hear
Every night with my ear.

And the window shakes at my head
    Over and over
And each little spring in my bed
Twangs with its brother.

And there thumps at the heart of the Hill
On the house wall – and runs
In the grass at the foot of the trees,
    The Reminder. The guns.

Enid Bagnold

For Celia Congreve, who served overseas with the Red Cross from late August 1914, the imagined sound of Mother Earth herself weeping for her sons, rather than the guns which she heard almost daily, provided inspiration for a poem that appeared in a 1915 anthology, *The Fiery Cross*, sold in aid of the Red Cross. Press baron Lord Northcliffe had commissioned Stephen Graham, a committed Russophile and extensive traveller in Russia, to write reports from Russia for *The Times*. On one occasion the exchange between a Russian friend of Graham's, one Vassily Vassilitch, and a Serbian officer was reported. This article proved to be the catalyst for Congreve's poem and was printed with it.

LAY YOUR HEAD ON THE EARTH'S BREAST

"Have you heard the earth crying?" said Vassily Vassilitch.
"What do you mean?" I asked.
"Why," said he, "I've heard her crying as I lay in the grass with my ear to the ground. I heard her. Like this, oo--m, oo--m, oo--m. It was the time the soldiers were being mobilised and women were sobbing in every cottage and in every turning of the road, so it may only have been that I heard. But it seemed to me the earth herself was crying, so gently, so sadly that my own heart ached." – Stephen Graham.

LAY your head on the Earth's breast and you will hear her crying,
Sobbing, softly, hopelessly, for her sons who are dead and dying.

Splendid and gay they are marching still to the music of bugle and band,
Bravest and best of my beautiful sons they are going from every land.

Are there none who will stay of all my sons? Must you all go?
Yes; all that you love, the pride of your eyes, Mother, you'd have it so.

Mangled and torn they lie in heaps, broken, dying and dead.
O scarlet blood of my splendid sons, you have dyed my green fields red.

What can I do for you, O my sons? My last, last gift is small,
A few poor sods to cover your heads and a scatter of snow o'er all.

Lay your head on the Earth's breast and you will hear her crying,
Grieving, softly, hopelessly, for her sons who are dead and dying.

Celia Congreve

The seasons in war poetry

The seasons allowed both professional and amateur poets to express feelings about the dislocated world they now inhabited. Many women poeticized the contrast between a world in which seasons follow their natural rhythms and the events unfolding overseas.

LINES WRITTEN DOWN IN DEVON JANUARY 1915

Startling it is to see the snowdrops blossom,
Startling to hear the throstle, once more, sing,
As though this year our hearts were tuned to harbour
The sights and sounds we used to love in spring.

O blood-drenched, alien fields in France and Flanders,
O graves unknown where our young heroes lie,
You hold our vision, you are our present, actual-
The near is distant, the remote is nigh.

Ella Fuller Maitland

Through summer, autumn, winter/And through spring: The seasons in war poetry

Amongst the bleakest of winter poets is Edith Mary Cruttwell. She refuses to believe, let alone take comfort from the idea of soldiers willingly sacrificing their lives for those at home. Despite the British facing no serious engagements in February 1916, continuous trench raids, sniper fire, shelling, and sickness caused by living in the troglodyte world of the trenches, meant the death toll continued to mount. The men's misery was unending, often intensified by seeing their comrades lying unburied in No-Man's-Land.

Cruttwell is aware of the increasingly unbridgeable gulf between those at home and those in Flanders. Two familiar farmyard objects prompted the following thoughts in February 1916.

TWO SCARECROWS IN THE SNOW

Two scarecrows lay across the snow,
    And I thought of the men across the sea,
Dark and silent and broken too,
    They lie in Flanders for you and me.

Two scarecrows lay across the snow,
    Broken and rent by the wind and the storm,
Ah, God, 'tis living bodies too
    That lie in Flanders and cannot get warm.

The scarecrows lie, dead battered things; –
    It seemed like a bitter blasphemy
(Like evil birds with tattered wings)
    That they should lie for all to see,

And take in vain the name of War,
    Too lightly have we passed them by,
The sacred name of our dead men
    And those of them who still must die.

Those scarecrows, stark across the snow,
    They are a cold, cold mockery,
They mock and mow and gibe at us
    Who dwell in safety across the sea.

     *   *   *

O bodies stiff, rest quiet now, –
    – But give us from the battlefield,
O spirits loosed from ragged shroud,
    The holy peace the snow can yield.

Edith Mary Cruttwell

The travesty of spring returning to a world at war provided American poet Sara Teasdale with the inspiration for this much anthologized poem. Rather than celebrate the arrival of spring with its promise of new life, she sees that it can only bring further horror. With increased hours of daylight the number of hours in which battles can be fought, and men can kill and be killed escalates.

SPRING IN WAR TIME

I feel the spring far off, far off,
    The faint, far scent of bud and leaf—
Oh, how can spring take heart to come
    To a world in grief,
    Deep grief?

The sun turns north, the days grow long,
    Later the evening star grows bright—
How can the daylight linger on
    For men to fight,
    Still fight?

The grass is waking in the ground,
    Soon it will rise and blow in waves—
How can it have the heart to sway
    Over the graves,
    New graves?

Under the boughs where lovers walked
    The apple-blooms will shed their breath—
But what of all the lovers now
    Parted by Death,
    Grey Death?

Sara Teasdale

Ethel Talbot Scheffauer's Easter poem is disturbing, subverting both pastoral images and the promises of the Christian festival; her foul images help to drive her message home.

EASTER 1918

The Lord is risen – – when shall they arise
Whose pale accusing eyes
    Glitter at night out of the marsh water
In the accursed lands?

In April come the flies,
    Following greedily the great slaughter,
With their bright eyes of jet
And long tongues always wet
    Following after the armies thick as sands.

And the birds come again – –
Not the small song birds, singing after rain,
    But they of stealthy flight,
    Following after the armies in the night,
The grey bird from the mountain in the east,
    The vulture and the kite.

And the small worms awake – –
    The little round worm and the slippery red,
They wake among the dead,
And gather up their numbers to the feast,
And drown in many a lake.
Where never a fevered beast his thirst may slake.

An evil, sullen pool – –
    Whose waters draining down into the earth
    Shall ready it for birth,
It is a rich grain, heavy and full,
Deep golden, long in the ear,
    Shall strike its roots into this fallow ground,
When all the guns are still, in some strange year,
When no man shall be forced against his will
To lift the sword and kill.

Now in the land of fear,
    Yesterday's cavernous hollow is a mound
Slippery with new death.

> The bells with iron breath,
>> Out of the cannon's mouth utter their verse,
>> Not blessing but a curse:
> Horror with blood upon her silken feet,
> Walks at broad noon across the dreadful hill
>> Where all the torrents meet.
> The Earth is bloody, like a murdered bride,
> The Lord is risen – – it is Eastertide.

Ethel Talbot Scheffauer

Even for those with little more than a passing knowledge of the First World War, 1 July 1916 resonates with meaning. At the end of this first day of the Battle of the Somme, Britain had sustained some 57,470 casualties, of whom 19,247 were killed. Many were the volunteers who had responded with such enthusiasm to the recruitment drives of 1914 and 1915. By the time the battle petered out in mid-November 1916, British and Commonwealth forces were calculated to have lost 419,654 dead, wounded and missing.

Although news of the Somme disaster filtered home relatively slowly, it soon became apparent that, far from achieving the hoped-for decisive break-through, the battle had resulted in overwhelming carnage. Through the losses sustained by the Pals Battalions, the heart had been torn out of many villages and towns, leaving whole communities bereft of young men. Winifred Letts is one of several women who contrast the ripening summer fields of 'happy England' with the blood-drenched fields of the Somme.

JULY 1916

Here in happy England the fields are steeped in quiet,
 Saving for larks' song and drone of bumble bees;
The deep lanes are decked with roses all a-riot,
 With bryony and vetch and ferny tapestries.
O here a maid would linger to hear the blackbird fluting,
 And here a lad might pause by wind-berippled wheat,
The lovers in the bat's light would hear the brown owl hooting,
 Before the latticed lights of home recalled their lagging feet.
But over there in France, the grass is torn and trodden
 Our pastures grow moon daisies, but *theirs* are strewn with lead.
The fertile, kindly fields are harassed and blood-sodden,
 The sheaves they bear for harvesting will be our garnered dead.
But there the lads of England, in peril of advancing,

Have laid their splendid lives down, ungrudging of the cost;
The record – just their names here – means a moment's careless glancing,
But who can tell the promise, the fulfilment of our lost?

Here in happy England the Summer pours her treasure
 Of grasses, of flowers before our heedless feet.
The swallow-haunted streams meander at their pleasure
 Through loosestrife and rushes and plumed meadow-sweet.
Yet how shall we forget them, the young men, the splendid,
 Who left this golden heritage, who put the Summer by,
Who kept for us our England inviolate, defended
 But by their passing made for us December of July?

Winifred Letts

Like many of her contemporaries, teenager Pamela Hinkson foresaw her own war-blighted future, her love and dreams buried beneath a stone.

A SONG OF AUTUMN

Was it only a year ago today
That you and I were happy, dear, together?
Not dreaming then how soon you'd haste away
And leave me lonely in the Autumn weather.

Not any more shall you and I go roaming
Along the hills we loved in wind and rain,
Stand in the storm to watch the wild birds homing,
Planning the future with no thought of pain.

Not any more shall you and I together
Wander along the sea-shore side by side,
Hearing the sea-gulls cry in stormy weather,
Yet knowing not the message that they cried.

Not any more shall we in bright June weather,
List to the streamlet running o'er its weirs,
As on that day when we two stood together
Not hearing in its music our own tears.

Not any more shall we in August weather,
Kiss the last kiss before I go alone
To tread the path which we two planned together –
My heart lies buried beneath a nameless stone.

Pamela Hinkson

If for Hinkson the autumn weather is reminiscent of all she has personally lost, Madeleine Stuart is aware how, in the first post-war autumn, the guns may have fallen finally silent but the physical and emotional burdens of the War continue.

AUTUMN IN ENGLAND 1919

I watch the reaper reaping golden corn
While the sun sets red and soft mists delay.
Where were you reaping, reapers, a year ago to-day?
I watch the reaper bind the sheaves at morn
While the haze hangs white on the moon's pale horn.
Where were you binding reaper, a year ago to-day?
In the fields of Mars, on the great highway
With the reaper Death, where the wounded were borne
Like burning sheaves from a furnace caught,
And the mist was fire and the stricken brave
Like shadows crept out from that living grave
Blind ... and life seemed death and death seemed naught.
And the fields were rank where the dead men lay
And that awful reaping ceased not night nor day.

Madeleine Stuart

Many poets construct their poem around just one season. For Beatrice Mayor summer, autumn, winter and spring represent the endless cycle of killing and dying, which for some on the Home Front seemed so far away as to be unimaginable.

SPRING 1917

It is spring.
The buds break softly, silently.
This evening
The air is pink with the low sun,
And birds sing.

Do we believe
Men are now killing, dying –
This evening,
While the sky is pink with the low sun,
And birds sing?

We do not.
So they go on killing, dying,
This evening,
And through summer, autumn, winter,
And through spring.

Beatrice Mayor

Conclusion: 'Nature turns faint'

During and indeed after the War, women poets exploited the pastoral genre to show how it had disturbed all previous certainties. Their erstwhile secure island had been violated. Death had descended from now malevolent skies, as the enemy targeted civilians. Although some poets strove to believe that soldiers fighting on foreign fields had been comforted by thoughts of their beloved homeland, and in their dying moments had glimpsed in their imaginations 'England, misty England', other poets were unconvinced by such platitudes.

Women who never left their native shores, knew that the boom of the guns on the Western Front now audible in England were, as Enid Bagnold commented, a constant 'reminder' of what was happening across the Channel. The 'guarding walls' that Rose Macauley felt those at home had built around themselves were no longer sufficient. Sara Teasdale and a number of other poets noted how although spring heralded new life, it also brought greater opportunities for killing. For Ethel Talbot Scheffauer even Easter, the most hopeful of religious festivals delivered not the promise of Resurrection but the assurance of corruption.

In their pastoral poetry, women make it abundantly clear that death, destruction and despair now lurked on both the Home and the War Fronts.

Chapter Four

'I've Worn a Khaki Uniform ... Significant Indeed': Serving Women's Poetry

During the Great War, over 100,000 British women joined the countless official and semi-official women's organizations established (or extended) to assist the war effort, many formed by women themselves. Some volunteered for a few hours weekly, others spent years overseas; a substantial number were within earshot of the guns for longer than many revered soldier poets and writers. Most felt, in Women's Auxiliary Army Corps poet I. Grindlay's words, that their 'khaki uniform' was 'significant', a visible sign of their contribution to the war effort.

Women's reasons for enlistment were varied: a number sought to escape hum-drum jobs or the boredom of their parents' drawing-rooms; others were motivated by patriotism and the conviction that they should assist their country in her hour of need. Some enlisted to avenge a man's death; some were pressurized by families keen to have a daughter in uniform, others defied their families by joining the embryonic women's auxiliary services. Former supporters of women's suffrage believed war service could hasten women's enfranchisement; others felt that if man must fight then woman must nurse. For many working women, the rates of pay and the conditions offered by the auxiliary armed services were attractive, with the added benefit of liberating them from the drudgery of domestic service.

A few women found themselves inadequate to war's demands, many discovered undreamed of reserves of character, courage and determination – and some also found that they could write poetry about their service, utilising the horror, humour, and even the mundane aspects of their lives.

Voluntary Unit poets

On 15 August 1914, when the War was only eleven days old, to the envy of their colleagues and indeed the majority of women, a small band of carefully selected uniformed women set off for the war zone. They were members of the Queen Alexandra's Imperial Military Nursing Service (QAIMNS) and its Reserve, (QAIMNSR). In England, women who already held Red Cross

Nursing certificates were desperately keen to don the uniform of one of the many volunteer corps, uniform being the visible sign of patriotism. For most, their ambition was, like that of male volunteers, to get to the war zone as quickly as possible.

Groups of well-meaning, privileged women, soon discovering that utter confusion reigned in the administrative midst of the Army Medical Service, founded and often funded their own volunteer units and simply went overseas independently to offer their services to Allied Medical Services. A number of them wrote poetry about their experiences 'at the Front' – not all of which was positive. Novelist May Sinclair's disastrous spell overseas is the subject both of the poem below and her 1915 *Journal of Impressions in Belgium*.

DEDICATION
TO A FIELD AMBULANCE IN FLANDERS

I do not call you comrades,
You,
Who did what I only dreamed.
Though you have taken my dream,
And dressed yourselves in its beauty and its glory,
Your faces are turned aside as you pass by.
I am nothing to you,
For I have done no more than dream.

Your faces are like the face of her whom you follow,
Danger,
The Beloved who looks backward as she runs, calling to her lovers,
The Huntress who flies before her quarry, trailing her lure.
She called to me from her battle-places,
She flung before me the curved lightning of her shells for a lure;
And when I came within sight of her,
She turned aside,
And hid her face from me.

But you she loved;
You she touched with her hand;
For you the white flames of her feet stayed in their running;
She kept you with her in her fields of Flanders,
Where you go,
Gathering your wounded from among her dead.

Grey night falls on your going and black night on your returning.
You go
Under the thunder of the guns, the shrapnel's rain and the curved lightning
    of the shells,
And where the high towers are broken,
And houses crack like the staves of a thin crate filled with fire;
Into the mixing smoke and dust of roof and walls torn asunder
You go;
And only my dream follows you.

That is why I do not speak of you,
Calling you by your names.
Your names are strung with the names of ruined and immortal cities,
Termonde and Antwerp, Dixmude and Ypres and Furnes,
Like jewels on one chain—
Thus,
In the high places of Heaven,
They shall tell all your names.

May Sinclair

Sinclair is unusual in publicly poeticizing the extent to which her foreign service had gone so dreadfully wrong and for the finger of blame she points at those whom she accuses of stealing her dream. Most women who felt antagonism towards colleagues only confided such deeply personal feelings to private journals or letters; they preferred, at least in their public writings, to voice admiration for their comrades, often in adulatory terms. However, much as Sinclair resented the way she had been treated by her colleagues and Hector Munro, she was haunted by what she had seen in Belgium and of Belgians' sufferings in the early days (and which continued throughout the War) as the Allied Armies hastened to evacuate, leaving that country to her fate. This poem, published in *The Egoist* on 1 May 1915, makes her feelings clear:

AFTER THE RETREAT

If I could only see again
The house we passed on the long Flemish road
That day
When the Army went from Antwerp, through Bruges, to the sea;
The house with the slender door,

And the one thin row of shutters, grey as dust on the white wall.
It stood low and alone in the flat Flemish land,
And behind it the high slender trees were small under the sky.

It looked
Through windows blurred like women's eyes that have cried too long.

There is not anyone there whom I know,
I have never sat by its hearth, I have never crossed its threshold, I have never

opened its door,
I have never stood by its windows looking in;
Yet its eyes said: 'You have seen four cities of Flanders:
Ostend, and Bruges, and Antwerp under her doom,
And the dear city of Ghent;
And there is none of them that you shall remember
As you remember me.'

I remember so well,
That at night, at night I cannot sleep in England here;
But I get up, and I go:
Not to the cities of Flanders,
Not to Ostend and the sea,
Not to the city of Bruges, or the city of Antwerp, or the city of Ghent,
But somewhere
In the fields
Where the high slender trees are small under the sky—

If I could only see again
The house we passed that day.

May Sinclair

Although for the majority of women nursing service took place on the Home
or the Western Fronts, a number of volunteers and professionals served in
more distant theatres. Mary Henderson worked as an administrator with the
Scottish Women's Hospitals (SWH), mainly in the Russia Unit. She dedicated
a poem to 'The Rank and File of the Scottish Women's Hospital' in response
to the Prefect of Constanza (Rumania)'s comment, 'No wonder Britain is so
great if her women are like that.'

Notwithstanding the hyperbolic language, this provides a vivid picture of the horrific conditions under which the women both travelled to and subsequently worked on the Eastern Front, caring for Serb and Rumanian soldiers – countries of which many had been ignorant before 1914.

LIKE THAT

'Like that.' Like what? Why British to the core,
You went beyond our sheltering British shore,
Out to the peril of an Arctic sea,
Bearing the flag of British Liberty.
You laughed above the lurking submarine,
Clothing Death's terrors in a happy sheen
Of debonair lightheartedness – I've seen
How very gallant women's hearts may be
Though torn the while with deepest sympathy,
British and women – women to the core.

I've seen you kneeling on the wooden floor,
Tending your wounded on their straw-strewn bed,
Heedless the while that right above your head
The Bird of Menace scattered death around.
I've seen you guiding over shell-marked ground
The cars of succour for the shattered men,
Dauntless, clear-eyed, strong-handed, even when
The bullets flung the dust up from the road
By which you bore your anguished, helpless load.
I've seen you, oh, my sisters, 'under fire,'
While in your hearts there burned but one desire –
What British men and women hold so dear –
To do your duty without fear.

Mary Henderson

Sinclair and Henderson concentrate their poetic attention on female comrades. Author turned volunteer nurse Mary Borden looks at the conditions in which the French *poilus*, many of whom would soon be her patients, were serving, conditions with which she was all too familiar. Heavy contamination owing to the extensive pre-war usage of fertilizers, the putrefying bodies and the thousands of gas shells that had been released across the lines, resulted in the ubiquitous mud of the battlefields posing as great a threat to the wounded as their initial injuries. Death by sepsis was common and nurses as well as soldiers were at risk from deadly infection.

AT THE SOMME: THE SONG OF THE MUD

This is the song of the mud,
The pale yellow glistening mud that covers the hills like satin;
The grey gleaming silvery mud that is spread like enamel over the valleys;
The frothing, squirting, spurting, liquid mud that gurgles along the road beds;
The thick elastic mud that is kneaded and pounded and squeezed under the
    hoofs of the horses;
The invincible, inexhaustible mud of the war zone.

This is the song of the mud, the uniform of the poilu.
His coat is of mud, his great dragging flapping coat, that is too big for him and
    too heavy;
His coat that once was blue and now is grey and stiff with the mud that cakes
    to it.
This is the mud that clothes him. His trousers and boots are of mud,
And his skin is of mud;
And there is mud in his beard.
His head is crowned with a helmet of mud.
He wears it well.
He wears it as a king wears the ermine that bores him.
He has set a new style in clothing;
He has introduced the chic of mud.

This is the song of the mud that wriggles its way into battle.
The impertinent, the intrusive, the ubiquitous, the unwelcome,
The slimy inveterate nuisance,
That fills the trenches,
That mixes in with the food of the soldiers,
That spoils the working of motors and crawls into their secret parts,
That spreads itself over the guns,
That sucks the guns down and holds them fast in its slimy voluminous lips,
That has no respect for destruction and muzzles the bursting shells;
And slowly, softly, easily,
Soaks up the fire, the noise; soaks up the energy and the courage;
Soaks up the power of armies;

Soaks up the battle.
Just soaks it up and thus stops it.

This is the hymn of mud-the obscene, the filthy, the putrid,
The vast liquid grave of our armies. It has drowned our men.
Its monstrous distended belly reeks with the undigested dead.
Our men have gone into it, sinking slowly, and struggling and slowly
   disappearing.
Our fine men, our brave, strong, young men;
Our glowing red, shouting, brawny men.
Slowly, inch by inch, they have gone down into it,
Into its darkness, its thickness, its silence.
Slowly, irresistibly, it drew them down, sucked them down,
And they were drowned in thick, bitter, heaving mud.
Now it hides them, Oh, so many of them!
Under its smooth glistening surface it is hiding them blandly.
There is not a trace of them.
There is no mark where they went down.
The mute enormous mouth of the mud has closed over them.

This is the song of the mud,
The beautiful glistening golden mud that covers the hills like satin;
The mysterious gleaming silvery mud that is spread like enamel over the
   valleys.
Mud, the disguise of the war zone;
Mud, the mantle of battles;
Mud, the smooth fluid grave of our soldiers:
This is the song of the mud.

Mary Borden

'Very Active Danger/Valiant And Determined': The VADs

Although there were multiple volunteer hospital and nursing units, the most
prominent, best-known and officially recognized volunteer nurses were
members of the Voluntary Aid Detachments (VAD). The majority of VADs
served via the Red Cross, a few were members of the Order of St John of
Jerusalem – they had identical status as the organizations merged to form the
Joint War Office Committee, the only difference was in the uniform volunteers
wore.

   Although these have often been magnified in novels and films, there were
some tensions between the professional nursing staff, the 'Pros', and the

VADS. With time, both sides learned to tolerate and value their respective contributions to the care of the wounded. Inevitably, these tensions found their way into poetry, as in this untitled poem written by Esther Bignold for her young VAD daughter Grace.

'Valueless A Duffer!' says the Sister's face,
When I try to do her orders with my bestest grace.
'Vain and Disappointing!' says Staff Nurse's eye,
If I dare to put my cap straight while she's walking by.
'Very Active Danger', looks the angry pro,
If I sometimes score a wee bit over her you know.
'Virtuous And Dumpy!' that's the way I feel,
When I'm uniformed from cap strings to each wardroom heel.
'Vague And Disillusioned' that's my mood each night,
When I've tried all day to please 'em and done nothing right.
'Valiant And Determined', I arise next day,
As I tell myself it's *duty* and I must obey.
'Very Anxious Daily' I await my leave,
Which I spend with my *own* soldier, as you may believe.
'Verily A Darling' that's his name for me,
When I meet him in my uniform of VAD.

Esther Bignold

In a poem published in February 1918, Marguerite Few focuses not on the chasm between professionals and volunteers but on the one separating VADs from their carefree, pre-war existence when a frenetic rounds of parties, balls and other social activities had been expected to culminate in marriage to a suitably eligible young bachelor, followed by motherhood. That world is now light years away from the one that the VAD in this poem now inhabits.

THE DÉBUTANTE 1917

Just 18 years and she has looked on death
And washed dread wounds and handled shattered limbs,
And sleepless watched nightlong a passing breath,
And seen strong men in agony – strange whims
Has humoured, choked her rising fears
And worked the harder that she shed no tears.

Her feet that should have danced are tired to-night
With pacing other measures many hours;
Her heart beats heavily that should be light,
For her no acclamations, feasts, and flowers,
But the long aching strain
Of waiting some lad who may not come home again.

So through the years I see her pass sublime,
The shadow of her sorrows on her face:
Poor child, the perfect mother for the race –
But old before her time.

Marguerite Few

VADs themselves wrote numerous poems about their service – indeed they were the most prolific of all uniformed women poets. Although some VADS served in tented Base or General Hospitals overseas (never in Casualty Clearing Stations), the majority served on the Home Front. They were always under the supervision of a professional nurse but, with the ratio of patients to professional nurses constantly increasing, additional responsibilities were handed to VADs.

Night duty was a time when volunteers' skills were often stretched to their limits; patients – and staff were at their most vulnerable with demons held at bay during daylight hours now surfacing to stalk the wards.

NIGHT DUTY

The pain and laughter of the day are done
So strangely hushed and still the long ward seems,
Only the Sister's candle softly beams.
Clear from the church near by the clock strikes 'one';
And all are wrapt away in secret sleep and dreams.

Here one cries sudden on a sobbing breath,
Gripped in the clutch of some incarnate fear:
What terror through the darkness draweth near?
What memory of carnage and of death?
What vanished scenes of dread to his closed eyes appear?

And one laughs out with an exultant joy.
An athlete he — Maybe his young limbs strain

In some remembered game, and not in vain
To win his side the goal — Poor crippled boy,
Who in the waking world will never run again.

One murmurs soft and low a woman's name;
And here a vet'ran soldier calm and still
As sculptured marble sleeps, and roams at will
Through eastern lands where sunbeams scorch like flame,
By rich bazaar and town, and wood-wrapt snow-crowned hill.

Through the wide open window on great star,
Swinging her lamp above the pear-tree high,
Looks in upon these dreaming forms that lie
So near in body, yet in soul so far
As those bright worlds thick strewn on that vast depth of sky.

Eva Dobell

One of the popular, albeit inaccurate, myths surrounding VADs is that all volunteers served in a nursing capacity. Many were cooks, scullery and ward maids, ironically perhaps as many would have been waited on by domestic servants in their homes. Some of those whose service was in the kitchen or pantry captured their new life in poetry, showing how the sheer reality of grappling with recalcitrant equipment could come close to lowering the spirits of even the most resilient of uniformed war workers.

This anonymous poet from Gallowhill Auxiliary Hospital, Paisley, (home of philanthropic Lady Smiley who would have been given the title of 'Commandant' and took a close interest in all that went on under her roof), vents her frustration with the kitchen range on New Year's Eve, whilst admitting that she is proud to be of service to wounded soldiers.

ODE TO THE KITCHEN RANGE

Old Range to you a bright New Year
Old thing, I almost called you "Dear"
Because the time is nearly here
    For us to part;
'Good-bye' I say without a tear
    With happy heart.

Your soot has often made me sneeze,
Your steel I've polished on my knees,
I've scraped some scores of spots of grease
    From off your top,
For four weeks now, Old Range, so please
    I want to stop.

Good-bye at five to sleep so sweet,
At earliest dawn we used to meet,
For you, my friend I had to greet
    About five thirty,
And on 'flue' days (twice weekly treat)
    You were so dirty.

Old Range, though you no more I'll clean
I hope till nineteen-seventeen
And though I send you, well, to Jean,
    There's no ill-will,
Because together we have been
    In Gallowhill.

Home of our wounded Tommies, where
I nurse, dust, cook – without a care –
Clean you Old Range, or turnips pare
    With Mrs. Plant;
There's one I bless because I'm there –
    Our Commandant.

Anonymous

   Despite the essential nature of their lowly tasks, these women who formed, according to the Gallowhill poet, 'the backbone of the nation', frequently felt overshadowed and looked down on by those who nursed the wounded. Winifred Wedgwood neatly sums up the differences between the VAD services in the following poem.

OUR VAD SCULLIONS

Our nurses are always apparent,
    So we give them their halos alright;

But how many think of our scullions,
　　Because they work buried from sight?

Yet their toil is hard and unceasing,
　　And often it's dirty work too:
But they cheerfully work without grousing,
　　For somebody's got it to do!

I liken them unto the stokers,
　　Who toil and are never seen.
Yet on them the whole ship's depending.
　　Now please stop – and – think – what I mean!

Winifred Wedgwood

'I wish my mother could see me now': Ambulance Units

The First Aid Nursing Yeomanry (FANY) was amongst the most decorated and successful of the women's units. Formed in 1907, the organisation aimed 'to provide assistance to civil and military authorities in times of emergency'. One form of assistance would be to gallop onto the battlefield to rescue casualties.

The realities of the Western, and indeed other Fronts meant that ambulances replaced horses. Having driven for the Belgian Army from the outset, on 1 January 1916, FANYs became the first women to drive ambulances officially for the British Army. Known to 'drive like bats out of hell' when travelling to collect the wounded, on the return journeys to hospital their patience, gentleness and consideration for those in their care was legendary.

Not only did they drive ambulances, they also maintained and serviced these vehicles themselves, and their mechanical skills were deeply respected. Sir Arthur Stanley, Head of British Red Cross Society, commented that members of the FANY had: 'The courage of a lion, the hide of a rhinoceros and a capacity so great that it could nurse the worst form of typhoid or start a frozen car.' They certainly needed all of these attributes.

Some FANYs poetically contrasted the humour and the harshness of wartime life with their pre–war existence. As the Corps recruited from amongst the most privileged strata of society, the differences between 'Then' and 'Now' were pronounced. This poet who terms herself 'One of the Saints', looks wryly back to her time as a débutante, comparing this to life in France during the grim winter of 1917-1918.

F.A.N.Y
(First Aid Nursing Yeomanry motor ambulance corps)

I wish my mother could see me now, with a grease-gun under my car
Filling my differential 'ere I start for the sea afar,
A-top of a sheet of frozen iron, in cold that would make you cry.
"Why do we do it?" you ask. "Why? We're the F.A.N.Y."
 I used to be in Society once,
 Danced, hunted and flirted, once!
 Had white hands and complexion once!
 Now I am F.A.N.Y.

That is what we are known as – that is what you must call,
If you want "Officers' Luggage", "Sisters," "Patients" an' all,
Details for "Burial Duty", Hospital Stores" or "Supply",
Ring up the Ambulance convoy, turn out the F.A.N.Y.
 They used to say we were idling—once,
 Joy-riding round the battle-field—once,
 Wasting petrol and carbide—once:
 Now we're the F.A.N.Y.

That is what we are known as, we are the children to blame,
For begging the loan of a spare wheel, and fitting a car to the same.
We can't even look at the workshop, but the Sergeant comes up with a sigh
"It's no use denying them *nothin'*!" "Give it to the F.A.N.Y!"
 We used to fancy an air raid—once;
 Called it a bit of excitement—once;
 Prided ourselves on our tin-hats once:
 Now we're the F.A.N.Y

That is what we are known as, we are the girls who have been
Over three years at the business: felt it and smelt it and seen –
Remarkably quick to the dug-out now, when the Archies rake the sky;
Till they want to collect the wounded, then it's "Out with the F.A.N.Y."
 Crank! Crank! You Fanys!
 Stand to your buses again –
 Snatch up the stretchers and blankets,
 Down to the barge through the rain!
 Up go the planes in the dawning!
 Up go the cars to stand by –

There's many a job for the wounded,
    Forward the F.A.N.Y

[Editor: *There is more than one version of this poem. This one is taken from Pat Beauchamp's 1919 autobiography* FANY Goes to War. *During air raids, personnel were supposed to shelter in dug-outs and over time they got used to sprinting towards these at breakneck speed. All the women willingly left their dug-outs when called on to drive the ambulances, even during an air-raid. 'Archies' was the name given to the large calibre anti-aircraft fire.*]

One FANY, Muriel De Wend, daughter of a retired colonel and sister of a young lieutenant who had been killed on 11 November 1914, worked with the St Omer Convoy. In a letter to her mother she describes one of the many ghastly nights during the winter of 1917, when she drove a windscreen-less ambulance through a hailstorm with 'the wind straight against us'. The hail was so severe that she thought that 'my poor face was bleeding'. Having to drive at four miles an hour in order to be able to see where she was going, the hail turned to snow and soon she 'could not see at all'. Throughout the drive, as she recounts in her letter, she was agonisingly aware of her fatally wounded passenger, who 'was conscious but dreadfully hit in the stomach, arms. I've got kind of numb at hearing people in agony but I think one hates seeing (these) dreadful sights more and more.'

Perhaps because only those who had driven in such conditions knew the full misery both for patient and driver, Ada Harris' poem focuses upon the ambulances themselves rather than the drivers. This poem also appeared in Pat Beauchamp's autobiography.

THE RED CROSS CARS

They are bringing them back who went forth so bravely.
Grey, ghostlike cars down the long white road
Come gliding, each with its cross of scarlet
On canvas hood, and its heavy load
Of human sheaves from the crimson harvest
That greed and falsehood and hatred sowed.

Maimed and blinded and torn and shattered,
Yet with hardly a groan or a cry
From lips as white as the linen bandage;
Though a stifled prayer 'God let me die,'

Is wrung, maybe, from a soul in torment
As the car with the blood–red cross goes by

Oh, Red Cross car! What a world of anguish
On noiseless wheels you bear night and day.
Each one that comes from the field of slaughter
Is a moving Calvary, painted grey.
And over the water, at home in England
"Let's play at soldiers," the children say.

Ada Harris

Women did not only drive ambulances. A very significant number drove vehicles for the army staff officers of both the British and Imperial forces. Initially figures of fun, many of those whom they drove came to respect their skills and request their services rather than those of a male driver. This poem, found amongst the Scrapbooks held in the Birmingham Public Library War Poetry Collection, had entertaining cartoon drawings to further re-inforce its point.

THE 'IF' IN THE CAR
With apologies to Rudyard Kipling

If you can get up early every morning
        When you would much prefer to stay in bed,
If you clean your car without a warning
        From the sergeant in command and not get 'fed';
If you can drive along in any weather
        And keep a cheery smile upon your face,
If you keep yourself in good boot leather
        When it wears out at a terrific pace;

If you can laugh when your car declines
        And holds up all the traffic on the roads,
If you can find the fault and it unravel
        Before the breakdown gang itself unloads;
If you can keep your hood from floating upwards
        In every breeze and gale that doth appear,
If you can keep your various broken footboards
        From slipping in and out your beastly gears;

If you can keep your radiator full of water
    When it's leaking out in gallons on the road;
If you can run all day without a slaughter
    Of a chicken! or a cow, perchance a toad;
If you can manage to digest your luncheon,
    In ten and a half minutes by the clock,
And be back again at your destination,
    Without receiving an electric shock;

If you can drive from nine o'clock till seven
    Every day of the long week and still live on;
If you can keep your temper until even,
    You deserve a putty medal nobly won!
If you can put up with each hardship,
    The weather, the passenger, your car,
And still keep bright – well all that I can say is:
    'You're a topper absolutely, nothing bar.'

The fact that these women could firstly drive and secondly afford to do so on a voluntary basis – and keep themselves in 'good boot leather' – provides a hint as to their elevated social status.

'For now I am a soldier': Poets in the Auxiliary Armed Services

In direct contrast to the privileged backgrounds of many VADs, FANYs, and members of organisations such as the Green Cross, the majority of women who served in the Women's Auxiliary Army Corps (WAAC), established in 1917 to 'free up a man for the 'Front' by performing domestic roles, were from the lower classes. They did not have the same access to publishers as more affluent women and almost certainly much of their poetry has been lost.

Only two WAAC poets' works appear in published volumes: I. Grindlay's *Ripples from the Ranks* is entirely based upon service life, whilst Brenda Bartlett avoids writing about her WAAC service (her work is considered in this book's last chapter). Hunting through personal documents and service magazines brings some to light and, like their sisters in other uniformed sections, these provide insight into their day-to-day lives and service.

Following the WAAC's foundation, the Press immediately suggested that their very presence would endanger the morals of the British Army. To try to dampen soldiers' ardour, the WAAC uniform was far from alluring but, for many women, the khaki-coloured coat-frock, clumsy looking shoes and round, brown felt hats provided a visible sign of their patriotic fervour.

MY ARMY HAT

My comrades sniff and sneer about my hat,
    Regarding it as a blemish on the Corps;
They cast aspersions on it from behind,
    And say it is disgraceful from before.
Their idle words do not excite my rage,
For there is no dishonour in old age.

For seven months now has it braved the blast,
    And, certainly 'tis somewhat worn and frayed,
Upholding not the beauty but the worth
    Of that from which an Army hat is made.
It is not yet by any means unfit,
And still must carry on and do its bit.

At any rate I would not change it now,
    Not even for a model from Paree.
Of envy for the sweetest hat on view
    My soul is most unutterably free.
'Tis old and scarred but what care I for that?
I'm very proud to wear an army hat.

(3617) I Grindlay

Other women became equally attached to both their uniforms and to their initially strange, militarized lives.

SOME WAAC

If you can smile when in your time "off duty"
You're told to go and do some beastly drill,
If you can joke when pinning on your brassard,
Although the colour makes you feel quite ill;
If you can jest when wearing Army stockings,
Beneath a dress nine inches from your feet,
Knowing that given 'half an earthly'
Your legs and ankles really are quite neat.

If you can grin when on your rare late morning,
You're wakened up to give your name and rank,

If on the pay you may (or may not) draw on Friday
You swagger round as if you own a bank,
If when you're told to fasten your top button,
You don't pass rude remarks about a "cheek";
If when you've got your frock so nicely gathered,
You don't mind putting back the pleat.

If you can laugh when down the main street walking,
The crowds of soldiers anything but mute,
You have to give (for all escape is cut off)
Your own inimitable rag-time jazz salute;
If you can stroll serenely onwards,
When Administrators and patrols are on your back;
If you can do these things and not get fed up,
You can bet your bottom dollar
You're SOME WAAC!

E M Murray

In case uniforms were not sufficiently unattractive to deter the opposite sex, fraternising was strictly forbidden, irrespective of the age or even occupation of the gentleman in question.

SMALL MERCIES

"Good morning," said the banker;
  "Good morning," I replied.
"A nasty day," he ventured;
  "Oh, not at all," I cried.
He gazed upon the landscape,
  And said, "I think it's wet";
"But very fresh," I told him,
  His puzzled frown I met.
"It's really beastly windy,"
  He challenged me again;
"But really very bracing,"
  I answered him. And then
The argument was finished,
  He handed back my book,
And once more said, "Good morning,"
  With quite an absent look.

"Good morning," I said brightly,
    And plodded through the rain,
Our intellectual converse
    Revolving in my brain.
For, since I am a soldier,
    'Tis seldom that I can
Permit myself the pleasure
    Of talking with a man.

(3617) I Grindlay

From March 1917, WAACs served in France alongside the Army Service Corps (ASC). Following an adverse (and entirely unfounded) attack in the Press on their morals, measures were put in place to restrict interaction still further. Often the first indication the men of the ASC gained of WAACs' arrival was an order to erect a barbed wire compound around the camp.

Women who had previously served in camps in England found the increased restrictions irksome. To compound the difficulties, following aerial attacks on WAAC camps in France in May 1918, trenches and dug-outs were constructed in order to offer some protection against such attacks. This Army Post Office clerk WAAC is far from alone in bemoaning the lack of male company and the physical restrictions. Like many others, she is not averse to pointing out the irritations of service in the Dannes–Camiers district whilst nevertheless recognising its joys.

From THE WAIL OF THE WAAC

If you're walking, call me early, call me early, Rosie dear
Tomorrow may be the happiest day of all the year.
For the Sergeants of the Ordnance are coming here today
And perchance their funny faces will drive dull care away.

Once my life was free from care, my smile a sight to see,
As to Signals I tripped gaily and poured out a cup of tea.
The Signals-master strafed me but I didn't care a jot,
But said to "Doings" Quickly go and bring another pot.

In my window boys would look, and smile as they passed by,
And when the spirit moved me, I would wink the other eye;

On the road I'd watch the Troops a-marching to and fro,
Whilst Dip and Rene pointed out the boys they'd like to know.

But now my lot is darkened and my temper's wearing thin,
For alas my view is all obscured by heaps of Sand and Tin;
And all around the office there are holes and wire fences,
And when 'tis dark you bark your shins or fall into trenches.

Gladys fell down one last night, no men were on the scene,
For if there had been they'd have seen her stockings coloured green;
And when I get back into Camp, pray what do I find there,
But Trenches, Dug-outs, buildings and changes everywhere.

…But when the war is over and we're safe at home once more,
We'll have many happy memories of the Q.M.A.A.C. Corps

'A[rmy].P[ost].O[ffice]. S.39.R.M.

June 15th 1918'

The women who served in the WAAC (subsequently the Queen Mary's Auxiliary Army Corps, QMAAC) outnumbered those who joined the Women's Royal Naval Service (WRNS) and the last-born, Women's Royal Air Force (WRAF). Poems by members of these two services are even rarer, although angst about the WRNS, their uniform and even their eagerness to enlist, appears in Mabel Beatty's parody 'The Walrus and the Carpenter'. This rather trivializes would-be 'Wrens' who flocked to the new service's HQ at Stanhope Street, London, where recruitment was underway, overseen by the service's newly appointed 'Admiral' or Principal Violet Waldy.

Members of both contemporary and present military services would recognize the endless administrative tasks, with individuals being referred to by their jobs rather than their names, and the acronyms that are part and parcel of service life.

THE WALRUS AND THE CARPENTER

The Sea Lord and the Admiral were walking
On the sand,
They wept like anything to see
So many men at hand;
"If women could be used instead"
They said, "it would be grand."

The sun was shining merrily
On 15 Stanhope Street,
The Wrens were busy bustling round
With eager black-shod feet,
With braided coats, three cornered hats,
They looked quite trim and neat.

"Oh women come and work with us",
The 'Admiral' did beseech;
With pleasant smile and full of guile
She made her opening speech:
We badly want your help ashore
(Correctly, on the beach)".

Then 4 young women hurried up,
All eager for the fray,
Their heels were high, their necks were low
(The fashion of the day),
"Shall we enquire at Stanhope Street
About the rates of pay?"

Four other women followed them
And yet another four
And thick and fast they came at last,
And more and more and more,
Until they reached from *Harrods
Up to Headquarters door.

It's very nice of you to come,
We wish you'd come to stay:
Perhaps you are a little 'old',
Or else a trifle 'gay',
Now this one here is 'just the type'
(This happens every day!)

"It seems a shame" young Waldy said,
To play them such a trick,
After we've brought them out so far
To turn them down so quick."

The A.D.P. said nothing but
"Their answers make me sick."

"The time has come", Recruiting said
"To talk of many things,
Selecting boards, enrolment forms
And whether wrens have wings."
"And whether dockets have them too"
Administration sings.

We weep for you," the others cried,
"We deeply sympathise."
With tears and sobs they sorted out
Those of the largest size.
Their tattered hieroglyphics swam
Before her weary eyes.

If seven wrens with seven pens,
Sat at them half a year,
"Do you suppose", the Admiral said
"That they could make them clear?"
"I doubt it," said the Deputy
And shed a bitter tear.

The moon was shining gaily down
On 15 Stanhope Street;
The Huns had given up their ships
"By order of the Fleet."
And when they asked what won the War
Their signal straight appeared,
"The Navy did its damnedest
But the Wrens it was we feared."

[Editor: * *The famous London department store Harrods is three miles from Stanhope Street.*]

Rivalries surfaced almost immediately within the various women's corps. When the Women's Royal Air Force was founded, a number of former WAACs 'deserted' to this new service, some undoubtedly enticed by the possibility of acquiring technical skills in aircraft maintenance and maybe, just maybe, learning to fly.

I. Grindlay is unimpressed by her colleague's defection to the WRAF – certainly considered (along with its male personnel) the most dashing of the three services, and warns of possible pitfalls. For Grindlay, soldiers are every bit as good as airmen.

TO I. CRUDEN

Go, dainty maid, your needle ply
Among those daring men who fly,
    But oh, my dear, be wary.
For compliments, like aeroplanes,
Are sometimes bent on hostile gains,
    Though sometimes the contrary.
You have a clear, well–balanced mind,
So need not be just too unkind,
    When offered some attention.
The good and bad you'll separate,
And not just rise to every bait,
    But surely I may mention,
That in our conversations here,
We may have been a bit severe;
    For 'mong our fighting brothers,
There is a black sheep now and then,
But most of them are good, brave men,
    The sons of noble mothers.

(3617) I. Grindlay

'The willing girls who plodded on the land': Women's Land Army

In July 1915, Maurice Hankey, Secretary to the War Cabinet, reminded colleagues that on his three recent visits to France he had been deeply impressed by 'the amount of work [done] on the land by old men, women and children'. Whilst not suggesting that Englishwomen should emulate Frenchwomen who, according to both photographic and written records, 'harness themselves into the rakes and wagons and pull them in the place of the horses – and they so seldom complain,' Hankey concluded, 'it would be a splendid thing if we could get the women on the land in this country too.' Cabinet members disagreed and initially little was done to get woman on to the land in an official capacity.

Nevertheless, by 1917 the food situation had reached crisis point. The government employed one of its favourite methods for hectoring the population: posters appeared instructing women to engage in National Service and 'Speed the Plough'. Recruiting rallies and agricultural demonstrations occurred up and down the land and those who wished to fight the food war became members of the officially recognised Women's Land Army (WLA) under the leadership of Lady Denman and Meriel Talbot.

Women were given a khaki uniform (unless working in dairies, where the chosen colour was white) to indicate that they too were soldiers. Long overshadowed by the Women's Land Army of the Second World War, these women were eager to contribute their labour and saw their service in patriotic terms.

TO THE TUNE OF KEEP THE HOME FIRES BURNING

We were summoned from the city, from the cottage and the hall,
From the hillside and the valley we answered to the call,
For we're fighting for our country as we till the fertile soil,
And our King and Country need our help and ask for earnest toil.
    Keep the home crops growing,
    In the soft winds blowing,
Though your work seems hard at times 'tis not in vain.
    Golden cornfields waving,
    Means your country's saving,
Golden sheaves at harvest time will the victory gain.

In the farmyard and the forest we are bravely doing our bit,
Some are milking cows for England, some th' giant oak trees split,
We are working for our country and we are glad to have the chance,
By increasing England's food supply to help the boys in France.
    Keep the home flags flying,
    England's food supplying,
Help to bring our gallant lads victorious home.
    Though the Germans raid us,
    English women aid us,
Keep our food stores fortified till the boys come home.

K M E Gotelee

However enthusiastic they might have been when they joined the WLA, women knew that their life would be transformed once their brief training was completed. This anonymous poet sums up what many women were feeling,

A LAMENT

I'm a-thinking and a-thinking of the Farm where I'll be sent,
Of the lonely little furrow where my days will oft be spent;
Of the harmless cows that poets say do naught but chew the cud,
Tho' I know when I go milking they'll be sure to have my blood!

I'm a-sighing and a-crying when I think of chilly morns,
Of creeping from my cosy bed to take the bull by horns;
Of goats that butt me in the back when I am off my guard,
Of stupid fowls and pigs and owls that squabble in the yard.

I'm a-moaning and a-groaning at the thought of beets and swedes,
Of digging beastly little holes and filling them with seeds,
Of planting all the luscious stuff that other folk will eat,
Of finding crumpled chicks and things beneath my spreading feet.

I'm a-grieving but believing, that I'll take the train to town,
That I'd rather see the streets pulled up than watch the grass mown down;
I'd sooner swallow Nestle's Milk than have to face a cow,
And much prefer to give up pork than have to keep a sow.

Anonymous WLA member

This anticipated loneliness was, in contrast to the lifestyle of the other women's services, a reality for many volunteers. Women were often sent to remote farms, frequently working amongst those who resented their labour; many farmers were sceptical about the Land Girls and their wives could be openly antagonistic.

However, by November 1918 many of the sceptics had acknowledged that, contrary to expectations, the experiment had been successful. One WLA member preserved this anonymous 'Tribute' amongst her archived papers:

A TRIBUTE TO THE LAND ARMY

What made our lives endurable when war with all its woes,
Was devastating countries, over-run by bitter foes,
Who tried their best to beat us by their frightful hammer-blows?
The cheerful girls who came out on the land.

Who kept us from repining then, while working morn till night,
We heard the big guns booming, although far away from sight,
Across the German ocean (so called but not by right)?
The smiling girls assisting on the land.

The girls who sang like skylarks when the sky was clear and blue,
The girls who to their sailors' or their soldiers' love were true,
The girls who helped to win the war as only girls could do,
The willing girls who plodded on the land.

The girls who fed the pigs, attended calves or milked the cows,
The girls who worked with horses, driving harrows, rolls of ploughs,
The girls who always peaceful, never joined in any rows,
The jolly girls who toiled upon the land.

The girls who kept on plodding to assist as maidens should,
To do the needful work that might ensure their country's good,
The man who fails to praise them must have brains like rotten wood,
Unlike the brains of girls who tilled the land.

In after years, when grandmothers these maidens have become,
They may inform their grandchildren (of whom they must have some),
How in the crucial days of yore, they made the farm work hum,
Those girls who helped to save their native land.

Anonymous

'Things which will abide': Precious memories

Perhaps more than for any other groups of women, those who had served in a uniformed capacity had experienced the greatest wartime disruptions to their lives. Often it was the support of colleagues that got them through the worst of times. Service life profoundly marked many women and they would take their experiences forward into their post-war lives.

AFTERWARDS

In course of time our drill we may forget,
The many turns and movements which we've striven
To perfect in ourselves and others, given
Much of our patience to – and yet
It will not matter, for even when we met
We knew this was not an end, but means
To help us better bear our part in scenes
Most varied, where our changeful work was set.

But there are other things which will abide,
The friendships made, the fellowship of our band,
The memories for us all of work and play.
The spirit which carries on whate'er betide,
The brave example of our leaders, stand
Within our hearts to cheer us on our way.

(Women's Volunteer Reserve Magazine, **March 1919)**

As time passed and women struggled to reintegrate themselves into civilian life, they sought to retain their links through Association Gazettes and newsletters which helped maintain contacts, kept members abreast of others' doings, and preserved memories. Some organisations went even further. The WAAC/QMAAC leadership, aware of the harsh, post-war lives of many former members, established several holiday venues. There ex-WAACs could spend time with former colleagues at little cost, reminiscing and offering mutual support as they adapted to a peace-time world which was not always empathetic towards women who had served.

'Shanghai' at Old Windsor in Berkshire was an early experiment – much appreciated by many ex-service women. One poet who gave herself the pseudonym 'Bristles' visited it when it was hardly finished. In time, many facilities including a camp superintendent were introduced.

From SHANGHAI

In the boiling grilling splendour of a summer afternoon,
I sat glaring in my window near the street,
I'd a "grouse" and proudly aired it and was wallowing in gloom,
With a sulky glance each friendly girl I'd greet.

For one was off to Margate and another going home,
A third unto the country she'd hied.
And here was I without a friend, with no fair lands to roam,
Condemned to stay in town at Whitsuntide.

I pretended not to see the fun, each girl was madly keen,
I sniffed a sniff and wiped a tearful eye
Reading (carefully inverted) a month old WAAC magazine
And longing to enjoy a real good cry.

While I idly glanced at "adverts" (Yes, old Grey is growing fruit,
And Brown A.A.'s a nurse I do declare).
I saw "Try Shanghai Camp, all loyal Waacs it's sure to suit" –
And suddenly it vanished, my despair.

So, I should have a holiday, oh! What a piece of luck,
Our "Ma'ams" have never failed us now or then,
So I wrote a little letter and I wrote with frantic haste
Till the words all spluttered ink from my pen.

In time I got an answer – "There's a camp down there for you,
If you don't mind joining four brave pioneers.
You'll have to do the work yourself, it's all quite crude and new",
I felt quite brave and gave three hearty cheers.

Then the camp had no *McClosky, no verandah and no punt,
When it greeted me that merry Whitsuntide.
As I "swatted" from the station for the place I had to hunt,
Cart a suitcase and a hold–all too beside.

When at last the pumping station showed its friendly bulk in sight,
I felt tired out, and sad, and almost done.
When a wild "War Whoop" from campers drew me quickly to the spot,
Where a good substantial tea had just begun.

"Did I see you once at Bostall?" D'you remember how Ma'am strafed?"
"I believe I met you once at Connaught Club."
Here are five good Waacs and merry, so we chatted and we laughed
As merrily the supper plates we scrub.

O! yarns and song and gossip, sitting underneath the stars.
Of dear dead days that never come again.
Those far, queer days when sorrow and when joy, they both were ours,
And the war was not all sorrow and all pain.

Sleeping out beneath the stars, or gathered round a table bare,
Spread with simple fare and flowers grown near by –
We're once again the care-free Waacs who'd done their little share,
To win the war and push the grey clouds by.

[Editor: * *Former WAAC McClosky was given the position of superintendent, which she filled admirably.*]

Some associations survived another war, folding only when many members had died. The longest surviving was that of the Scottish Women's Hospital (Royaumont Unit) whose members had served at the Abbaye de Royaumont in France. It was mourned by the few frail survivors on its closure in 1973. 'It's just that I have outlived everyone I ever worked with ... I among others miss the newsletter, it is a tender link and keeps us informed,' wrote one former member. Their flimsy letters, (which a few women donated to archives, sensing an historical importance reaching beyond the sad catalogue of rheumatism and influenza), their cherished *Gazettes* and the poems they wrote, provide powerful evidence of the strength of servicewomen's bonds.

Reading this preserved correspondence, it is hard not to be moved to tears by the strength of feeling and sorority between these now elderly women who, like old soldiers, jealously guarded memories of those indescribable, distant days and still recalled what VAD Lesley Smith called their 'four years out of life' when they served at the Abbaye de Royaumont

ROYAUMONT SONG

1

Do ye ken Royaumont, and the old high tower?
And the engine-house with its one-horse power,
And the cloisters calm in sun and in shower,
And the Blessés out there in the morning?

Yes I ken Royaumont and the jolly old crew,
The Doctors all in their uniform blue,

Sisters and chauffeurs and orderlies too,
And the *rab-rabiaud* in the morning.

Chorus
For the sound of the name to the heart brings a thrill,
And the spell that it cast, it is over us still,
Could we forget, even had we the will,
Royaumont, Royaumont in the morning?

2

Do ye ken Royaumont, and the Chief whom we love?
Compound supreme of the serpent and dove.
With Joffre and Pétain and Foch hand in glove,
And the pride of us all in the morning.

Yes I ken Royaumont and the blessed Curé
Trudging his twelve kilometres a day,
And the smile on his face as he used to say,
"Royaumont, c'est ma vie!" in the morning.

Chorus
For the sound of the name ... etc. etc.

3

Do ye ken Royaumont, and the gallant Poilus
Black, white, and brown, in the *horizon-bleu*
And the wonderful things that they used to do,
In the day and the night and the morning?

Then here's to Royaumont with my heart and soul,
And here's to *V.C. which was half of our whole,
And here's to every name that is writ on the roll,
And loved Royaumont in the morning!

[Editor: * V.C. Villers-Cotterets was a SWH advance hut or field hospital about
65km from Royaumont and close to the Front. Many Royaumont personnel did
a spell of duty there and in 1918 worked under shell-fire during the German
advance. Joffre: French Chief of Staff until December 1916, replaced by Pétain
who was moved sideways in May 1918 and was subordinated to Allied Supreme

Commander Foch. Pétain played a relatively minor role in the remainder of the war.]

'We were summoned from the city, from the cottage and the hall'

The opening line of K Gotelee's poem to the Women's Land Army applies to all the uniformed women of the Great War. Many socially privileged women marched out of their parents' drawing rooms to volunteer as nurses, ambulance drivers, and orderlies. Some travelled thousands of miles from their native shores to succour the wounded and comfort the dying. In so doing, some lost their lives and a few became legends in their own lifetime.

Other women needed to earn their living. With husbands, fiancés, boyfriends, brothers and friends wearing His Majesty's uniform, they discovered that it was up to them to step up to the mark and demonstrate patriotism and determination. Although life might not always have been easy 'now I am a soldier', camaraderie, commonality of purpose and the need to rise to the National Emergency and free a man for the Front, enabled them to accept, or at least find covert ways round, the restrictions that curtailed their liberty (and often their fashion sense).

By 1917, with thousands of tons of foodstuffs being sunk by enemy shipping, every acre of land had to be cultivated. Now it was women's duty not only to prepare food in such a way that no crumbs were wasted, it became incumbent upon them to help to produce it. They responded to Lord Ernle, President of the Board of Agriculture's plea to provide 'the food bullet' and ensure that the country was not starved into submission.

As the war that people had imagined would be over by Christmas 1914 stretched into months and years, women from all walks of life responded to their country's 'stirring call for [wo]men' and through their uniformed service played a decisive role in helping to secure victory. And with victory finally secured many in the post-war world turned to those amongst whom they had served to keep alive precious memories of those days when they had done their 'little bit' to win the War.

Chapter Five

Giving Sorrows Words: Grief in Women's Poetry

Grief and mourning are, unsurprisingly, dominant themes in women's wartime poetry. The ways in which poets present these themes often provide insights into how women negotiated the death of a loved one. Many women took comfort from concepts of chivalry and sacrifice, maintaining, as they would do into the 1920s and beyond, their belief that this war was fought to save civilisation. Others reject these concepts; the horrors had been so great, the grief so total that they sought and found new language in which to confront their disintegrating world.

Poetry shows women adopting, adapting, sometimes rejecting, established mourning tropes and traditions, as they seek to come to terms with slaughter on a scale that would have been inconceivable a decade earlier.

'Lending grief its sad ostentation': Mourning wear in grief poetry

In the nineteenth century, clothing outwardly signified bereavement and mourners' respect for the deceased. In the Edwardian era, assistants in department stores as well as etiquette books guided the newly-bereaved through every aspect of fashionable mourning. Black garments were supposed to shield wearers, primarily women, from the public gaze and there was a certain security in adhering to well-established codes of conduct and behaviour. These, like so many other areas of life, would almost immediately on the outbreak of war, undergo seismic shifts.

When the War was barely one week old, and no casualties had yet been sustained, a Joan Seanton suggested to *The Daily Mail* that it would lower morale should black be worn for those killed in action. With insight into rising food prices, she felt that it would be better for the poor to buy food than mourning wear; however, she seems to have overlooked how many of the makers of mourning clothes were indeed 'the poor'. The correspondence that ensued was but the opening salvo in a long-running battle fought in the letter columns of national and local papers, about the desirability or otherwise of wearing what Hamlet so bitterly referred to as 'The trappings and the suits of woe'. Poets including Constance Maynard also entered the lists.

WATCHING THE WAR

Feel as you will,

Let there be no expressing,
Streets filled with black

Would be far too depressing.
Mothers and wives

Leave your anguish unspoken,
Silence! wear colours,

With heart and life broken.

Constance Maynard

If mourning wear was discouraged in England, in Germany a prohibition relating to mourning clothes seems to have been strictly enforced. However Constance Maynard accepts that such clothes provide many mourners with psychological benefits.

MOURNING IN BERLIN

Comfort is found
In every nation
In lending to grief
Its sad ostentation.

Constance Maynard

If mourning rituals helped some of the bereaved cope, externally at least, other poets were equally convinced that a public show of grief would lower the morale of soldiers home on leave. Violet Spender's admonition to remain outwardly cheerful masks deep sorrow for her own brother Albert, who was killed at Ypres on 20 November 1914. (Alfred Schuster's name is on the Menin Gate, as his body was never found.)

IN MEMORIAM A.F.S.

Life he did gladly give
Who much rejoiced to live
And, beyond all on earth,
Loved her who gave him birth.
Then prize the gift he gave
Ye, whom he died to save!
See things as with his sight:
Feel some of his delight
In works of God and man:
The books he liked to scan,
The pictures, culled with care,
His home, the open air,
The friends he loved to greet
With understanding sweet,
With whom he gladly shared
The joys for which he cared
Till ever, bright and brave,
That last great gift he gave!
* * * * * * *
God! Help us bear the cross
We take up with his loss,
Nor let our faces sad
Make other folks less glad.
Rather with voices gay,
Cheer them upon their way
Giving whate'er we can

Violet Spender

"Oh Son, oh Child": Interments and maternal grief

In all cultures, some ceremonial farewell to the dead occurs and by the outbreak of the War, funerals in Great Britain had become elaborate undertakings; the more elaborate the funeral, the greater the apparent respect for the dear departed. During the War, if death had followed a period of hospitalisation rather than occurring on the battlefield, some family members were able to attend funerals on either the Home or Western Fronts (the latter not infrequently at government expense).

Nevertheless, the majority of the bereaved were deprived of any final leave-taking. Newspapers sought to reassure mourners that battlefield interments were dignified and photographic evidence of soldiers' funerals near the Front was supplied. However, not all were convinced by the media coverage of wartime interments.

THE DEAD

The battlefields are grey and scarred
Beneath the quiet sky;
Oh! Though the earth be stony hard
'Tis there the dead men lie.

Not under friendly English grass,
In the soft clay at home;
But tumbled in a bloody mass
Together in one tomb.

Shell and shrapnel, gas and flame,
Their burial service were;
Each had a name but no man's name
Is on his sepulchre.

Each had a name but each man's name
Is melted into one –
Wiped out by shrapnel, gas and flame:
And each a mother's son!

Margaret Sackville

By the early part of the twentieth century, falling infant mortality rates meant that for the first time in human history, parents had reasonable expectation that their children would outlive them. As hostilities continued, although parents may have anticipated a son's death, grief for their child was naturally overwhelming.

In their poetry, the majority of mothers frame sons' deaths and interments in heroic discourse, amongst them Alexandra Grantham who takes some comfort from envisioning her son's funeral, following his death in combat during the evening of 28 June 1915 on the Gallipoli Peninsula. Her imaginings are far removed from the reality of this most bitter of campaigns but, in the opening lines of this sonnet, written weeks after 20-year-old Hugo's death, she has captured the peacetime atmosphere of early morning Helles, a place she had undoubtedly never visited.

SONNET XXXI

Superb the sun arose from sapphire sea,
Flung forth sheer gold on cliff and olive hill,
While western islands lay in slumber still,
There at the Dardanelles they buried thee.
Thy grave in a dewy nullah they had made,
Tenderly they laid thy wounded body low,
Solemnly commended thee to God, then slow
And sad moved off – ended work of priest and spade.

And as to morning duties back they turn,
For ever from speech with thee passed quite away,
Who knows, whilst spreading sunbeams hotter burn,
What glorious dawn of what stupendous day
Breaks in thy tomb, on what immortal quest
Has soared the soul they deemed at perfect rest?

Alexandra Grantham

[<u>Editor</u>: *Grantham refers to Hugo as 'thee' not in some archaic or pretentious use of the language but, as a native German-speaker, she would have used the familiar form 'du'* [thou] *to address her child.*]

The psychology of grief and mourning has been widely studied in the twentieth century and it is known that mothers who cannot recover their child's body will go to considerable lengths to find out details of his or her last moments. Army padres were often inundated with requests, pleading to know if their son had sent a last message. As a hospital letter writer in France, May Bradford encouraged moribund soldiers to mutter a few words that she could relay to their families. Nurses strove to transmit patients' final words, aware that these would give comfort in the long months ahead.

Despite such efforts, many mothers envied the woman who had been by their son's side, listening to his last words and holding his hand as he died.

THE WOMAN AT HOME

Each at her post we stand.
Mine is the safer, easier part
And yet there is an iron band
Of envy round my heart

For her, the weary nurse who spent
Those last dear moments at his side,
The woman who in pity bent
And kissed him when he died.

Amelia Josephine Burr

This lack of farewell also weighs upon the mind of Private Harry Coxford's mother.

IN MEMORIAM

Somewhere in France our hero sleeps,
Somewhere in England his mother weeps,
Could we have heard his last farewell
The grief would not have been so bad
For those who loved him well.

Sleep on dear son in a soldier's grave
A grave we may never see,
But as long as life and memory last,
We will always think of thee.

Mrs Coxford

In Christian tradition, the dead are buried as close to their home as possible; in 1914, the local churchyard was still the favoured final resting-place for beloved family members. This was a way of keeping them within the family fold. Twenty-four-year-old Private John Vincent Toye was killed in Gallipoli; his mother felt that her grief would have been lessened had he been buried near to his family in Londonderry.

IN MEMORY OF PRIVATE JOHN VINCENT TOYE 10028 KIA 2-7-1915

Had he reached home though sorely maimed
Our own precious dear
And friends stood round his bedside as the end
Was drawing near.

* * * * * * *

Some comfort then we could have got
We knew where he was laid
Bedecked the gravetop with our tears and keep
It bright arrayed.
* * * * * * *

Each evening as the sun went down
We could have wandered there
And bending low before our god
Have said a silent prayer.
* * * * * * *

Until we meet on heaven's bright shore
We bid adieu for evermore
Till all our earthly sorrows cease
God rest his soul in peace.

Sarah Toye

Sarah Toye's grief was such that when records were being compiled by the City of Derry War Memorial Committee in October 1926, she appended a handwritten copy of the poem to the form that the bereaved were sent to ensure that their loved one's name was accurately recorded on the memorial. She requested that this be kept in the book of record; this wish was respected and it remains there to this day.

Not being with her eldest son Hugo as he died also caused Alexandra Grantham great anguish, as this poem, published in her local newspaper three weeks after his death, makes plain:

TO MY SOLDIER SON

I could not fold thy stricken hands
I could not close thy broken eyes,
Nor smooth thy hair, nor kiss thy brow
Too far, too dead thy body lies.
No mother's care to tend and watch.
But thou was first amongst the brave,
Thy headstone Glory and God's Love
Resplendent on thy soldier's grave.

Alexandra Grantham

Perhaps to ease their pain, some mothers cast their poetic minds back to happier times when their child was safe at home with them. Alys Trotter remembered a carefree 1909 cycling holiday in Picardie with her 14-year-old son and 16-year-old daughter, oblivious to the fate that awaited Nigel at La Fosse, near Béthune, in October 1914. Like Grantham, she addresses her son directly as a way of helping to keep his memory alive. Naming and speaking to the dead, as well as recalling their virtues, is therapeutic in grief work.

'PICARDIE'

There's a pathway through a forest in the Picardie I know,
A port where girls haul up the boats with men and fish in tow,
And the hills run down to the market town where the country-women go.

And behind it is the village, and the coast-line lies below,
And down the road, the dusty road, the carts ply to and fro
By the stately frieze of forest trees beyond the old Chateau.

There were three of us on bicycles upon the road that day,
You wore your coat of hunting green, and vanished down the way.
"Le petit Chasseur, la mère et soeur"*, we heard the women say.

You vanished as a speck of green among the shadows blue,
And children trudging up the hill stood still and called to you:
"Le petit Chasseur, qui n'a pas peur"**, they laughed and called to you.

O boys, you wield a bayonet now and lift the soldier's load!
O girls you've learnt to drive the plough and use the bullock-goad!
But the hunter's laid, still unafraid, near the trodden Béthune road.

There's a pathway through the forest in the Picardie I know,
And O I'll dream and wander there; and poppy fields will glow;
And I'll watch the glare of the dusty air where the market wagons go.

Alys Fane Trotter

[Editor:* *'The young Hunter, his mother and sister'*]
[Editor: ** *'The young Hunter who has no fear'*]

Whilst many mothers poeticize their own sons, there is a significant body of poetry by women who imagined that the War was stealing their future motherhood. Professional nurse Nina Mardel anticipated what grief psychologists call an 'empty pathway' stretching ahead. Believing that she will never be a mother, she seeks comfort from her deep Christian faith.

I SHALL NEVER FEEL

I shall never feel
The clasp of little arms about my neck –
A soft form cradled near my empty heart,
Oh ravening cruel need! There is no want,
They say but has its purpose in God's plan.
Yet I could sob my very life away
For empty heart – and empty mother-arms.
Day wears to day! I try to fill my life
With work, ambition, helping other's pain,
But when wide-eyed through the long night I yearn,
My very self one burning aching want,
I can but kneel with useless arms outflung
And feel his gentle hand upon my head,
And kiss His garment's hem and pray for strength
To live my life and lock the inner door.

Nina Mardel

'Seldom they enter into song or story': women's deaths

A predominant theme of women's grief poetry is the loss of a son. Bizarrely, no preserved poetry appears to relate to a daughter's death, although there are some prose tributes to dead daughters ranging from letters preserved in archives to the occasional memoir published by grieving parents. Even if mothers bereaved of daughters rarely if ever took up their poetic pens, women's deaths inspired some poetry.

Unsurprisingly the first female death to be poeticized was that of Nurse Edith Cavell. She was executed in October 1915 for having contravened the neutral status of medical personnel and assisted British soldiers to escape from occupied Belgium. In the heightened atmosphere of the time and the ensuing outrage, no poet explores the illegitimacy of her actions and the legality of the execution. Using hyperbolic religious language, war-monger Helen Key glories in Cavell's so-called 'martyrdom'. One cannot help but feel that Cavell herself would have been deeply uncomfortable with the sentiments Key portrayed.

EDITH CAVELL

Weep for her sigh for her cry for her? No!,
She has shown how closely a woman may go
Up the mountainous path of the wayfaring Christ
To keep with her Captain her wonderful tryst.
She has shown how boldly a woman may soar
Through the scud and the storm to the warmth of the shore;
She has shown how proudly a woman may die –
Clean truth on her lips, clear faith in her eye.
To think on her name is to thrill and to glow
But weep for her, sigh for her, cry for her, No!

Fight for her, ache for her, wake for her? Yes!
Brothers! This murder is yours to address,
Butchered by bullies at dead of the night,
Alone and defenceless she fought her last fight.
Our Empire of ages, our lordship of seas
Could give her no wages, could win her no ease –
But hot foot for vengeance her Brothers will press –
Ache for her, wake for her, break for her? Yes!.

Helen Key

Similarly hyperbolic, although not bellicose in tone, Mary Henderson captures in verse the military funeral of Dr Elsie Inglis, the founder and inspirational leader of the Scottish Women's Hospital (SWH). Inglis died from cancer in November 1917, the day after she returned to England from serving in Russia. Crowds thronged the Edinburgh streets for a last glimpse of Scotland's heroine.

IN MEMORIAM ELSIE MAUD INGLIS

Scotland has gathered you, dear daughter, to her breast;
Beneath the shadow of the Castle Rock you passed to rest.
Yet we who followed in that long, long line
Of those who came to honour at the shrine
Of one who held her life a little thing,
Loving her country and her country's king,
Her country's honour and her country's name,
Loving its glory, bitter for what shame

Might blur the brightness of Great Britain's fame –
We know you are not dead.

The hands, indeed,
So quick to minister where there was need,
The hands we loved, may not touch ours again,
May not alleviate our mortal pain;
They lie quiescent in the hands of God.
Yet we who followed when your footsteps trod
Beyond our Island shores, who knew your quick
Instinctive action for the helpless sick,
Your clear-voiced answer when there came the call
For succour from a Nation like to fall,

Who saw that undulled radiance in your eyes
Given to those with whom 'the Vision' lies –
We know that in that Flag-protected cask,
Lies but the weariness of her whose Task
Grown greater than her tired mortal frame,
Bears her beyond the greater strength and fame.

Mary Henderson

Other women mourned poetically for those whose service had inspired them, even if the life lost made little subsequent mark on history. Sister Mary Gray served with the SWH at Royaumont in France from its earliest days. Following an operation for appendicitis in January 1916, she died on 23 January. One can only wonder if her death, like that of American Nurse Helen Fairchild who died in France in January 1918, was caused by her exposure to the gas she would have inhaled when tending patients.

Mary Gray, like most nurses who died on active service, was buried with full military honours. SWH Nurse Mabel Jeffrey was amongst the uniformed mourners and the funeral inspired the poem below.

IN MEMORIAM

In the midst of this time of stress and strife,
We mark the end of a peaceful life.
Filled to oe'r flowing with loving deeds
With selfless efforts for others' needs.

No mourning crowd with its black array,
But our workaday garb of blue and grey,
As we troop in silence over the crest
Of the hill to take her away to rest.

A simple service of praise and prayer,
The notes of a hymn in the open air,
Her country's flag, white flowers and green,
Tokens of thanks for the life that has been.

The thunder of guns comes over the hill,
As we march away from the churchyard still,
With faces lifted yet hearts bereft –
Carry on in her footsteps the work she's left.

Mabel Jeffrey

Like many soldiers, women's war-related deaths also occurred at home. Many uniformed women exhausted by war service succumbed either to the 1918-1919 Spanish 'flu epidemic or the many complications of the illness. One was Women's Volunteer Reserve Colonel Lilian Sutherland whose comrades appear to have felt her passing very deeply.

BEREAVED
(on the occasion of Colonel Sutherland's funeral)

God's ways are rarely our ways. We bow to his decree
Perforce, while yet we wonder, Lord, why must this thing be?
So well-beloved, so young, so fair 'tis mystery to me
Why we should be bereft of her. Lord, why must this thing be?
Perchance Thine ends are better served by taking her to Thee:
We can but mourn with earth-blind eyes; Lord, why must this thing be?
Still let us strive to "carry on", it may be she will see,
This discipline may serve to bring and keep us nearer Thee.

March 5 1919

325 Birmingham

Not only individual women's deaths were poeticized. Agnes S Falconer memorialises her compatriots who, in 1915, were amongst the first to die overseas.

SCOTTISH NURSES IN SERBIA

Their eager, helpful hands, their love and lore
Eastward they carried to War's frowning keep:
Fever, War's daughter, met them at the door.
And kissed them to their sleep.

O, sometimes she is tender when she slays!
Haply she lent them, through her drifting dreams.
Loved voices, Scotland's primrose-blazoned braes,
Cool songs of homeland streams.

Death takes his toll — the young, the bright, the brave —
Europe's proud nations in his net lie snared:
But these hands — weaponed not to smite but save —
How ill can these be spared!

Agnes S. Falconer

On her way to nursing service in Malta in late 1916, VAD Vera Brittain visited the graves of Canadian Army Nursing personnel, Matron Jaggard and Nurse Munro. They, like so many of their patients had died of sickness whilst stationed at Lemnos, on the Greek island of Mudros, the final resting-place of countless Gallipoli veterans.

THE SISTERS BURIED AT LEMNOS
("Fidelis ad extremum")

O golden isle set in the deep blue Ocean,
With purple shadows flitting o'er thy crest,
I kneel to thee in reverent devotion
Of some who on thy bosom lie at rest.

Seldom they enter into song or story;
Poets praise the soldier's might and deeds of War,
But few exalt the Sisters, and the glory
Of women dead beneath a distant star.

No armies threatened in that lonely station,
They fought not fire or steel or ruthless foe,

But heat and hunger, sickness and privation,
And Winter's deathly shill and blinding snow.

Till mortal frailty could endure no longer
Disease's ravages and climate's power,
In body weak, but spirit ever stronger,
Courageously they stayed to meet their hour.

No blazing tribute through the wide world flying,
No rich reward of sacrifice they craved,
The only meed of their victorious dying
Lives in the hearts of humble men they saved.

Who when in light the Final Dawn is breaking,
Still faithful, though the world's regard may cease,
Will honour, splendid in triumphant waking,
The souls of women, lonely here at peace.

O golden isle with purple shadows falling
Across the rocky shore and sapphire sea,
I shall not picture these without recalling
The sisters sleeping on the heart of thee!

HMHS 'Britannic' Mudros October 1916

Vera Brittain

Although a few medical women have entered into song and story – poetic silence appears to surround the deaths of all other women, including the countless munitions workers who lost their lives through their service.

'Brother of mine': Brothers in sisters' poetry

By the late nineteenth century, strong bonds were developing between siblings in middle-class families. Wartime writings from this social group corroborate these findings. Poems for lost brothers are frequently poignant.

Mary Boyle was left with a 'paralysing sense of daily loss' when her much younger brother David was killed at Le Cateau on 26 August 1914 – one of the very first engagements of the BEF. Having shared a past, she now feels that his death has stolen away her future.

SONNET V

Sometimes I hear your footstep on the stair,
A curious way you scuffled slippered feet,
And am inclined to run halfway and meet
You on my threshold. Waiting in my chair,
Grow cold, whilst thinking you were really there,
There was no pause before you came to greet.
A laugh, an extra scuffle, movement fleet
To silence protest, light pull of my hair
To tilt my face so eyes could laugh at eyes;
The mirror would reflect two faces gay.
Instead it shows a woman staring blank.
Whose ears are traitors, telling wished for lies,
Whose eyes are blinded, looking far away
Unto last August when her youth's sun sank.

Mary E Boyle

Boyle's belief that her brother's death has destroyed a part of her is far from unique. Girton graduate Kathleen Montgomery Wallace's brother, Basil Coates, was killed on 7 September 1915. A number of her poems are based upon the Cambridge she will never again explore with Basil and, like Boyle, she anticipates an unshared future in which dreams will never be fulfilled. She is far from alone in finding little comfort in the ubiquitous platitudes offered.

BECAUSE YOU ARE DEAD

Because you are dead so many words they say.
If you could hear them, how they crowd, they crowd!
"Dying for England – but you must be proud."
And "Greater Love" – "Honour" – "A debt to pay."
And "Cry, dear!" some one says: and some one "Pray!"
What do they mean, their words that throng so loud?
    This, dearest, that for us there will not be
Laughter and joy of living dwindling cold;
Ashes of words that dropped in flame first told;
Stale tenderness made foolish suddenly.
This only, heart's desire, for you and me,
We who lived love will not see love grown old.
    We, who had morning-time and crest o' the wave

Will have no twilight chill after the gleam.
Nor any ebb-tide with a sluggish stream;
No, nor clutch wisdom as a thing to save.
We keep forever – and yet they call me brave! –
Untouched, unbroken, unrebuilt, our dream.

Kathleen Montgomery Wallace

Although we tend to think of Great War as a young man or woman's war, bereaved siblings were not always young. Sybil Bristowe was forty-seven when her 42-year-old brother Private Vivian, serving with the South Africa Medical Corps, was killed.

TO HIS DEAR MEMORY (APRIL 14TH 1917)

Beneath the humid skies
Where green birds wing, and heavy burgeoned trees
Sway in the fevered breeze,
My brother lies.

And rivers passionate
Tore through the mountain passes, swept the plains
O'er brimmed with tears, o'er brimmed with summer rains,
All wild, all desolate.
Whilst the deep Mother-breast
Of drowsy-lidded Nature, drunk with dreams
Below Pangani, by Rufigi streams,
Took him to rest.

Beneath the sunlit skies,
Where bright words wing, and luxuriant trees
Sway in the fevered breeze,
My Brother lies.

The bending grasses woo
His hurried grave: a cross of oak to show
The drifting winds, a Soldier sleeps below,
– Our Saviour's cross, I know
Was wooden too.

Sybil Bristowe

[Editor: *According to a footnote to the poem, on the night Vivian died, 'the river Rufigi rose so high that none of his battalion could cross it to attend to his last honours'.*]

Like Bristowe, Katherine Mansfield also saw her beloved brother's death in terms of Christ's sacrifice. Her grief for Lieutenant Leslie Heron Beauchamp was overwhelming:

TO L.H.B (1894-1915)

Last night for the first time since you were dead
I walked with you, my brother, in a dream.
We were at home again beside the stream
Fringed with tall berry bushes, white and red.
"Don't touch them: they are poisonous," I said.
But your hand hovered, and I saw a beam
Of strange, bright laughter flying round your head
And as you stooped I saw the berries gleam.
"Don't you remember? We called them Dead Man's Bread!"
 I woke and heard the wind moan and the roar
Of the dark water tumbling on the shore.
Where--where is the path of my dream for my eager feet?
By the remembered stream my brother stands
Waiting for me with berries in his hands...
"These are my body. Sister, take and eat."

Katherine Mansfield

'My grief untold': Disenfranchised grief in women's poetry

An inability to speak about, let alone declare their love in public, lack of official status, or even shame, complicated some women's grief work. Being neither wife, sister, mother, nor fiancée, these women had sometimes to hide their grief from the world's prying eyes. They were what grief psychologists call 'disenfranchised mourners'.

Well-known poet Eleanor Farjeon was one whose grief could be termed 'disenfranchised'. She had kept secret her love for Edward Thomas and appeared to be little more than a close family friend. When she received news of Edward's death from his widow Helen, she had naively hoped that Helen would be able to comfort her. The two women met in London before travelling together to the Thomas home in Epping Forest. Eleanor realised that she would need to be strong for Helen's sake and in a poem called 'The Outlet' she explores how she spent a considerable amount of time with the grieving family, before going 'away my grief untold.' It would be several weeks before Farjeon could begin her own grief work, much of which she captured in a series of elegiac sonnets – although Thomas is never explicitly named.

The relationship depicted in Olive Downes' 'Friends Only' appears less complicated than the Farjeon/Thomas one, nevertheless the speaker realises that her mourning will be overlooked by those with a more obvious claim to the deceased's memory. This lack of status places additional burdens on those forced to grieve silently and alone.

FRIENDS ONLY

We were just good pals together, and partners, you and I
At tennis, dancing, badminton, in days now long gone by;
Stage lovers too we often played but as friends and nothing more,
We parted when you went away to play the game of war!

I do not think you kissed me, even, I wish you had, my dear!
'Twould have helped me keep my courage through this long and lonely year
    —For ah! I *knew*
I loved you then; yet had to see you go
Without one word to tell me if you loved me too, or no!

Now where grey ships keep silent guard across the northern sea,
Somewhere you lie and with you there, the dearest part of me!
But I'm neither wife nor sweetheart, so I may not weep, my dear,
Or seem as if I missed you, even, when other folks are near.

Olive Downes

Another group of women whose grief had to remain totally concealed were mistresses. In the sexually-charged atmosphere of the war years, there would, inevitably, have been a number of them. This 'courtesan' is jealous of the wife who has the right to grieve, and although she acknowledges she has 'wronged' the wife, she experiences despair at the loss of the man she too loved.

Although this courtesan may be imaginary, similar sentiments have been found within very personal papers in archives such as the Peter Liddle Archive at the University of Leeds.

COURTESAN

This thing is theirs.
Those other women,
they have it for their own.
Theirs is the right to pride,
the right to grief.

Those other women, women of men's houses,
Where children may be —
I have made mock of them.
And now this thing is theirs.

Theirs is the road and theirs the field,
as always was the house.

For them the men go out upon the road.
And to each one of them
if her man fall,
belongs the field wherein he lies.

The burden of the war is theirs to bear,
and bearing it they have a right to sing
of love and death and glory,
honour and faith and sacrifice,
exultantly.

Is the house fallen?
Theirs was the right to fall with it.
The men go out to battle.

Those other women have the right
to laugh them off
and weep for them after.

And I, I have no right
to even look upon it.

Helen Mackay

Other contenders for soldiers' love have also seemingly been written out of family history and poetic record. In their idealised published memoirs, a number of mothers from socially privileged backgrounds portray themselves not as the remote, hierarchical figures they would have been in their sons' lives but as their constant companions. Nannies, entrusted with the care of sons and, of course daughters, are unmentioned, yet the grief these women felt would have been deep, as this anonymous poem found in a scrapbook, makes poignantly plain.

THEIR NURSES

We rocked their blue-lined cradles, we watched their smiles and tears;
With toil-worn hands we led them along the helpless years;
They brought to us their sorrows, to us their broken toys;
We were their first fond mothers, they – just our baby boys.

The years went by. From Sandhurst, clean-limbed broad-shouldered men,
To us in lodge and cottage would come our boys again,
In from a long day's hunting or wet walk with the guns,
To take their tea with "Nana". These were our grown-up sons.

Then came the calling bugles that drew them as with chords;
Our boys came home as soldiers in buckled belts and swords;
'Twas "Wish me luck, then, Nan; I'm off to join the crowd!"
What luck we did not wish them! And oh, but we were proud.

We shared their every hardship; we knew, we knew how well
The boys we nursed would bear them in face of shot and shell;
By Memory's fireguard shadow flung o'er a white cot's fold,
We with the hearts of mothers, knew when our boys slept cold.

We shared their every triumph admired as from afar
Each new toy as they showed it — each medal, clasp and bar;
Our babes were grown to Captains; we saw them crowd the lists
With wooden swords of boyhood held firm in dimpled fists.

At last, long feared and waited, the casual word came through:
We knew them "killed in action"; no more their mothers knew;
The world may speak of motherhood; we felt its pangs for these
Who learned to play at soldiers long since beside our knees.

Their medals to their mothers — the honour and the pride;
We, too, with arms as empty, remembering, have cried;
They were our dimpled babies whose laugh and lisp we keep;
We watched their infant cradles — God guard their soldier sleep!

Anonymous

'I want thee now': Frustration and condemnation

In the decades preceding the Great War, young women were expected to remain chaste until marriage. In affluent families, young women's interactions with the opposite sex were closely monitored and chaperoned. Being seen alone with a young man could cause irreparable damage to a woman' reputation and even destroy her chances of making a 'good' marriage. Whilst it was recognized that a young man would almost certainly be unable to control his sexual urges, that a young woman might also experience desire was to be ignored at all costs.

One of the most surprising features of women's grief verse is their poeticization of physical desire. Even as early as 1915, a number of grief poems have a strong sexual subtext:

REMEMBERING

Love, sweet & joyous, and laughing came to me,
Welcomed mid hours of toiling, long and drear,
Love who had seemed so precious in my sight.
And oh! He came so near and yet too near
Perchance, for now the joyless morning light
Brings toil alone ... that means no time for fear,
Thank God! Nor time for yearning and regret.
Oh! all day long I can forget, forget!
But always I remember in the night.

The days that were of summer born, and fled
Too soon; the tenderness, the joy, the faith,
The purpose, and the longing and the might
Of youth's clear passion have made tryst with death.
Because of blindness where God meant more light,
Because of following a mocking wraith,
The sun of love hath swiftly, sadly set ...
Oh, all day long I can forget, forget
But always I remember in the night.

All day there is the ardour and the claim
Of life's demands, the feverish race to win.
There is but dark and silence in the night,
And memories of passion without sin,
Too sweet for music and too dear for light.
And there is time to go back and begin
Remembering all ... Love claims so great a debt. ...
Oh all day long I can forget, forget!
But always I remember in the night.

Violet Gillespie

As the war years lengthened and the sexual atmosphere heightened, cases of sexually transmitted diseases (often euphemistically dubbed 'It') increased, with significant numbers of soldiers being hospitalized. Women were seen as placing soldiers at risk, draconian laws were introduced via the Defence of the Realm Act (DORA) and so-called purity campaigners entered the fray. One was a deeply religious middle-aged novelist who used the pen name Beatrice Chase. Bereft of her fiancé, she began campaigning to promote soldiers' chastity and, naturally, that of the women they left behind. She encouraged men to become 'White Knights' and join the Great [Chastity] Crusade, assuring them that she would pray for all those who signed the 'pledge' to be 'pure and noble' and 'protect women [who] have fallen too low to protect themselves'.

Chase's volume of poems published in 1916 has few offerings that would be termed' war poetry', although her underlying feelings about chastity, chivalry and women's part in a man's undoing come across in one or two pieces, the most notable in a poem entitled 'To_____'. She advises her subject to 'refuse to be lured to sin by any siren: this alone is Chivalry.'

Perhaps feminist Helen Hamilton had heard of this 'Great Crusade' and was unimpressed by the perceived hypocrisy of those who expressed concern about the loosening of sexual constraints.

PRUDES IN A FRIGHT

"Oh no! We never mentioned It,
        Before the War,
        We prudish folk.
Too nice-minded I assure you,
And awfully moral, don't you know!
But now we shout it from the roofs,

We choke it down fastidious throats,
    We chat about it in the home,
    And mention it to Bishops.
        Yes really!
And boys and girls, young men and maids,
We hunt with fearful zest,
To whisper warnings in their ear:
Beware my dear young innocents,
Beware we do entreat you,
        Beware of It.

That dread disease we once ignored,
    And rightly,
For all its blighting devastation,
    It was too horrid,
        Too improper!
And more, unyieldingly maintained,
    Stern in our sense of rectitude,
    And strict decorum, sore affronted,
That those who fell a prey to It,
    Those sexual sinners,
    Worst of sinners,
Should have no remedy supplied,
    If we could help it!
    Let them suffer,
The innocent no less than the guilty!
    Assuage the chastisement of God!
        How blasphemous!
        How impious!
Moreover, we were told that It,
Destroys to all eternity,
    The Soul immortal."
(How though, destroy what cannot die?)
        "Go to!
Such questions are beside the point.
    We know the truth
    And state it.
But now as our good allies say,
    *Autres temps, autres moeurs,**
    The War, you know –

What could we do?
Men who otherwise could die
     For us you understand –
A noble satisfying fate, you'd think,
     Get It instead.
     Disgraceful!
     Dreadful!

We *must* have soldiers,
     Strong defenders,
     Cannon-fodder,
     Whatever happens!
Suppose the Germans won,
     Where should we be?
So out with all the remedies,
Let no-one be without:
March every woman straight to gaol,
     Seen talking to a soldier!
Nor will we ever cease to scream
To scream our very loudest,
     At men and maids,
     At boys and girls,
     Beware, beware,
     Oh do, do, do!
     Each of the other,
          Lest It …"

"Oh dear, but will they listen?
We *must* have soldiers,
Strong defenders …"

     Must you?
     But why?

Helen Hamilton

[Editor: * Translation: *'Other times, other customs'*]

Despite the best efforts of Chase and others, sex remained in the air and one
of the most surprising features of women's grief verse is their poeticization of

physical desire. A considerable corpus of poems admit more or less openly to sexual frustration. QMAAC Brenda Bartlett's poetry is at times erotic, as she combines sex and death in a frenetic *danse macabre* and appears to criticize those who advocate chastity. In wartime's heightened sexual atmosphere, Venus willingly becomes the lover of Mars, the relationship is consummated joyfully:

TOO WELL

And so they tell us we have loved too well,
Too well! Not even the meaning of the words
Is known to those who glibly cast them at
Our joy-crowned heads, O dearest heart of mine!
Their little puny souls will never know
One tithe of the passion that has held
Up to the level of the ancient stars
Our feeble clay, and brought us to the moon
High-swinging in the sky, and got beyond
The barriers of time and space,
Because we loved – too well!

And yet they tell us we have loved too well,
And go upon their placid blameless way,
And thank their God they are not such as we.
Our gods are wind and ocean, stars and sky,
And all familiar, unfamiliar things,
And we in turn will bless them, hands upraised
In thankfulness, that come what may, we've lived!
We who have known the glory of the gods
And in one night have tasted Hell and Heaven
Because we loved – too well!

And so they tell us we have loved too well,
And Hell will be our portion after death –
But if together surely Hell were heaven,
And if we've sinned, then both have sinned alike.
And we will face them proudly, knowing that,
If still together we can bravely face
The worst Hell knows with jest upon our lips!
But we have only sinned in loving deep,

And yet may see the shining courts of Heaven
Because we loved – so well!

Brenda Bartlett

A few bolder poets are prepared to admit, unashamedly, to sexual longings; the more inhibited ones nevertheless hint at these. One modest touch remains in much of the poetry that suggests sexual frustration, many women only refer to their soldier lover by his initials. In one of the War's many gender inversions, they may be protecting his reputation as much as their own.

Margaret Furse married weeks before war was declared. Several of her poems show that she is aware of how the newly bereaved can be caught up in what grief psychologists term 'bondage' to the dead.

CAPTIVITY

Once it was freedom that you gave,
    And then your eyes
Were as lake waters, deep and grave,
    Holding the skies.

I leaned to drink and had no fear
    Or thieving doubt;
Loving thee so brought heaven near,
    Shut sadness out.

Now when the passionate inward fire
    No longer sleeps,
Fain would I stir with fierce desire
    Those silent deeps.

Fain would I drink – and yet I stand
    A prisoner here –.
Myself withholds my eager hand,
    I go not near.

Margaret Furse

Several bereaved women wrote in diaries and memoirs of their attempts to move on with their lives following war bereavement, accepting that they had a life or at least a half-life of their own to live. Popular novelist May Aldington poeticizes a young woman who holds her feelings at bay by day, but in the silence of the night, finds controlling her emotions harder to achieve.

AFTER

It has taken so long to forget you –
So long to put out the flame
Shall I ever forget your kisses
Or cease to thrill at your name?

Thro' the day not a thought will I give you,
The passion of work is my all.
I will heed not the sea waves murmur,
I will hear not the Spring bird's call.

But oh! There's the night to follow
The spark of the flame alarms;
And I ache in a speechless sorrow,
For the memoried touch of your arms.

And I pray in the silent darkness
Which hides my love in its shame,
That God will let me forget you,
The prayer is a sob – and your name.

May Aldington

A much younger poet, Joan Rundall, is not alone in hoping that however overwhelming her grief, memories might sustain her should the worst happen through the long years ahead.

THE FARM OF THE APPLE TREE

I saw you standing by the gate,
I heard you call to me
With the wind cry and the bird cry and the far-off cry of the sea.
Was there fire in your eyes that they could light
Such a fire in the heart of me,
When the young moon sailed from amber clouds
O'er the Farm of the Apple Tree?

A light from the window flashed and leapt
Through the night in a golden stream,
With the moonfire and the starfire and the fire of a world a-dream;
But I only saw your burning eyes
Implore me silently,
And felt your hands upon my own
By the Farm of the Apple Tree.

A night, a day, a night
You gave your love to me
With the wind love, the bird love and the wandering love of the sea;
You left me roaming a world of pain,
With a space alone set free
Where my remembered fires for ever sleep
In the Farm of the Apple Tree.

You woke the life within my life,
My soul from her sleep of years.
You lighted a lamp in the World for me that is blinding my eyes with tears,
But you left a dream I cannot lose
Of fire in the heart of me,
And in the touch of your hands upon my own
In the Farm of the Apple Tree

Joan Rundall

One woman whose tragically short-lived marriage was soon only a dream was Elsie Paterson Cranmer. Her poem 'Premonition' proved prescient:

PREMONITION

Suddenly out of the cold and mist and gloom,
A gleam of silver moonlight –*you* were there
Beside me in the little narrow room
Smiling your old glad familiar smile
Full of sweetness.
                    With a secret fear
That this was some poor shadowy wraith of you
I touched your eyes … and then we mutely kissed,
Not with the fiery kisses as of old,

But a sad dumb pitiful clinging.
        For a while
No word was said until you suddenly drew
Yourself away from me. Your eyes grew cold
Your mouth implacable ....
        Strangely you fled
Away into the cold and gloom and mist,
And then I knew – I knew that you were dead.

Elsie Paterson Cranmer

Widowed within three weeks of her marriage, Cranmer recognizes how, to the sexually innocent, her grief has an incomprehensible dimension.

MAID VIRTUE*

Fragile and slim and pale is she,
And cold as cold virginity.
She cannot feel the passionate pain
Of dreaming hearts, that dream in vain.
The crimson pleasures of the Wise
Only fill her with soft surprise.
Fragile and slim and pale is she
And cold, as cold virginity.

Elsie Paterson Cranmer

[Editor:* *Almost certainly her betrothed but unmarried sister.*]

Cranmer herself is amongst *The Living Dead*, – the title of her deeply moving collection. What Samuel Taylor Coleridge in *The Rime of the Ancient Mariner* had memorably termed 'Death-in-Life' was now Elsie and the approximately 160,000 War-widows' mate.

REMEMBRANCE

I shall remember. When the years have flown
Away, and left no single visible trace
Of all your beauty and your body's grace
And you are one with the earth and sky and air.

I shall remember how my heart grew cold
Beneath the sea-cold chilliness of your own,
And dumb, with the sick dumbness of despair.

And when the last faint, shadowy evening light
Of life departs from me – when comes the night,
And I am feeble grown, and frail and old,

I shall be taken from the haunts of men;
Oh, heart I loved, I shall remember – *then*.

Elsie Paterson Cranmer

Whilst we associate war widows with young women, older women were, of course, also bereaved. Just occasionally, a middle-aged wife lifted the veil on her mourning and hinted that she too was suffering the loss of her sexual partner as well as, in Alexandra Grantham's case, needing her husband to comfort her after the loss of their eldest son.

SONNET IV

My dead, my dead, O my beloved dead!
What gifts would I not bring to fate to hold
Your strong warm hands again, to enfold
You in my arms, soothe the wounds from which you bled,
Hear the rich music of your voice, see
The kindling happiness of your old smile,
Speak with you 'twixt lingering sobs and laughter, while
You kiss'd my tears away, and comfort me.

My dead, my dead, O my beloved dead!
Each night I long for you on lonely bed,
That in bright spirit-land of sleep my pain
Be ended, you living in my dreams again.
You never come – Can you not hear me weep,
You loved ones, or is your slumber all too deep.

Alexandra Grantham

Most of these poets were writing and grieving on the Home Front. In one of a series of untitled, unpublished sonnets, written at her hospital in France, Mary Borden's perspective is different. How can she, as a blood-spattered nurse working so close to the front line and dealing with the most horrifically injured men, remain attractive to her soldier-lover?

> No, no! There is some sinister mistake.
> You cannot love me now. I am no more
> A thing to touch, a pleasant thing to take
> Into one's arms. How can a man adore
> A woman with black blood upon her face,
> A cap of horror on her pallid head,
> Mirrors of madness in the sunken place
> Of eyes; hands dripping with the slimy dead?
> Go. Cover close your proud untainted brow.
> Go quickly. Leave me to the hungry lust
> Of monstrous pain. I am his mistress now.
> These are the frantic beds of his delight—
> Here I succumb to him, anew, each night.

Mary Borden

Although for some war bereaved, comforting words assisted them in coping with, even accepting the death of the beloved, others found the euphemisms insulting. They yearned for the beloved's strong, virile body and words gave little solace. However asexual the public representations of war grief, in their poetry many women moved beyond chaste love, giving us insight into the sexual reality of female war bereavement. These intensely private, intimate poems differ from the public face of grief, with its asexual love for virtuous knights and from the need for public remembrance.

'It's over, over, it's the end'

News of the Armistice was greeted by many with jubilation; for others it was a bleak reminder of all that they had lost. In a diary entry for 28 September 1918, Cynthia Asquith, daughter-in-law of former Prime Minister Herbert Asquith, notes that now that the 'world has stopped spinning', it would be hard for the bereaved to come to terms with the fact that the 'dead were not only dead for the duration of the War but forever'.

May Wedderburn Cannan was working in a government office in Paris when news of the Armistice broke. But not everyone had a reason to celebrate:

THE ARMISTICE
IN AN OFFICE, IN PARIS

The news came through over the telephone:
All the terms had been signed: the War was won:
And all the fighting and the agony,
And all the labour of the years were done.
One girl clicked sudden at her typewriter
And whispered, 'Jerry's safe', and sat and stared:
One said, 'It's over, over, it's the end:
The War is over: ended': and a third,
'I can't remember life without the war.'
And one came in and said, 'Look here, they say
We can all go at five to celebrate.
As long as two stay on, just for today.'

It was quite quiet in the big empty room
Among the typewriters and little piles
Of index cards: one said, 'We'd better just
Finish the day's reports and do the files.'
And said, 'It's awf'lly like *Recessional,
Now when the tumult has all died away.'
The other said, 'Thank God we saw it through;
I wonder what they'll do at home today.'

And said, 'You know it will be quiet tonight
Up at the Front: first time in all these years.
And no one will be killed there any more,'
And stopped, to hide her tears.
She said, 'I've told you; he was killed in June.'
The other said, 'My dear, I know; I know …
It's over for me too … My man was killed,
Wounded … and died … at Ypres … three years ago …
And he's my Man, and I want him,' she said,
And knew that peace could not give back her Dead.

May Wedderburn Cannan

[Editor: *'Recessional' a poem by Rudyard Kipling was very popular during the War.]

For bereaved women, the fact that their own loved one would not be coming home made the Peace celebrations particularly bitter:

ARMISTICE DAY

The crowds are dancing in the street below,
I hear their happy, dancing feet, I know
That Peace and Victory have come to-day.
But I – I cannot dance and sing as they,
For all my soul is darkened with despair,
And close beside the hearth I've dawn your chair.

The banners that bedeck my window-sill
        Fly out like phantoms in the gas-lamp's flicker,
Strange sounds and voices are about to-night
        And eerie shadows make the heart beat quicker.
What if your feet, your eager, running feet,
Were running up my stair!
What if I suddenly turned my head
And in the doorway you were standing there!
*   *   *   *
God! how the firelight flickers on the empty chair!

Marjorie Kane Smyth

American Florence Van Cleve is aware that far from women rejoicing together that the War was now finally over, the joy of those whose loved ones were returning would be a constant reminder to the bereaved of all that they had lost.

From MATER TRIUMPHANS

What can I say to you? I hide my joy
As though it were a crime; I would not be
So cruel as to flash the jewel-light
Of this my rapture on the saddened sight
Of your poor tear-dimmed eyes.
        To me Peace means,
Blissful renewal of a love that lives,
Made dearer stronger, by the memories
Of absence, and by faith now justified;

But you!
        To you it means a Golden Star*;
Eternal silence of the well-loved voice;
A shadowy presence hovering in the home
That once was his and yours to break your heart
With longing, and to salt your bread with tears.

What can I say to you? There is no way
For Rapture to communicate with grief;
I Have and you Have Not; and that is all!
How can you bear the tumult and acclaim
When come the great grey ships from overseas
Bringing his comrades to their waiting homes?
Has Heaven any solace for your soul?

Florence Van Cleeve

[Editor:* *The US Government awarded war bereaved mothers a Gold Star, but not all found this a comforting or suitable recompense for their son – or daughter's life.*]

Margaret Sackville looks beyond the grief of those whose loved one will not return. She anticipates how bereaved mothers, women who had suffered at the hands of enemy soldiery, and those who had worked for the war effort would become an embarrassment to a world eager to move on. In peacetime they would become inconvenient reminders of dislocated years.

VICTORY

Who are ye that come with eyes red and weeping,
        In a long, long line and silent every one?
See overhead the flag of triumphant sweeping –
        "We are the mothers and each has lost a son."

Cries of the crowd who greet their god of glory!
        What of these who crouch there silent in the street?
"We are outraged women – 'tis a common story,
        Quietly we lie beneath your armies' feet."

> Red flags of conquest, banners great and golden! –
>> Who are these silent ones upon our track?
> "We in our thousands, perished unbeholden,
>> We are the women; pray you, look not back."

Margaret Sackville

Personal and Public Memorialization

As early as 1915, a Graves Registration Commission had been established to ensure that the burial places of those killed in action were duly recorded. Under the inspired leadership of Sir Fabian Ware, this commission would become the Imperial, subsequently Commonwealth War Graves Commission, whose dedicated work continues to this day.

Many women, however, wanted to create a different, more personal kind of memorial to their loved one, and verse was their chosen medium:

I WILL A TOMB UPRAISE
(Written on learning that my boy's body was left unburied on the field of battle near Gaza)

> I will a tomb upraise to thee, my son,
> A tomb to weather every earthly storm,
> Whereon no stone shall crack nor rust may form,
> A tomb that shall defy the years that run.
> Yea though thy bones may rot – all that was spun
> Upon the web and loom of thy young life,
> Thy flesh and beauteous form, features that knife
> Of Fate carved fine which were at birth begun –
> Still on that sacred soil thy tomb shall rise;
> I pile it up for thee in loving verse,
> O may it be eternal as the skies.
> Though thy dear dust doth everywhere disperse,
> Still, still may mother-love with fire divine,
> Cleave more than marble for the hallowed shrine.

Mrs Tyrrell-Green

Although in time, bereaved, 'superfluous' women did become, as Margaret Sackville had anticipated, if not an embarrassment then at least an inconvenience, initially, women and especially mothers were given priority in the rituals which marked the end of hostilities and commemorated the dead. On 11 November

1920, an unusual and elaborate ceremony took place in London's Westminster Abbey, the burial of the Unknown Warrior. According to *The Times*, official invitations were extended to one thousand of the mothers and widows who had applied to attend. Their 'seats of honour paid for in grief', these women were considered guardians of the nation's sorrow.

The elaborate staging and ritual resembled nineteenth century state funerals, yet this was the burial of an unknown soldier – not necessarily an officer, perhaps even a private. The man's anonymity and this symbolic act of committal were intended to comfort those mourning the 704,803 British personnel who had perished in this Great War for Civilisation. For many, this burial did indeed provide comfort, even closure. A leap of the imagination allowed the bereaved to imagine that maybe, just maybe, their own soldier now rested amongst kings, poets and statesmen.

THE NAMELESS DEAD
(Armistice Day 1920)

In the packed streets the women's eyes are red, –
    Those hungry eyes of starvèd mother-love,
That strive to pierce the coffin lid above
    The nameless envoy of the nameless dead.

"Missing so long!" young widowed memories cry, –
    O those unending nights of lonely tears!
Those tortured hopes. These furtive ambushed fears!
    Is it for *my* beloved the people sigh?

Whose shattered body they have brought from far, –
    From blood-soaked trench and love-untended grave,
To crown with honour in that honoured nave –
    Victim at once and victor of the war.

Muriel Elsie Graham

Not all women were convinced that the Abbey, with its splendour and grandeur, was the appropriate final resting-place for 'their' beloved.

REMEMBRANCE DAY IN THE DALES

It's a fine kind thought! And yet – I know
The Abbey's not where our Jack should lie,
With his sturdy love of a rolling sky;
     As a tiny child
He loved a sea that was grand and wild.
     God knows best!
Near-by the sea our Jack should rest.

And Willie – Willie our youngest born –
I fear he might be lonesome, laid
Where the echoing, deep-voiced prayers are said, -
And yet the deep-voiced praying words
Reach God's heart too with the hymns of the birds.
     In His keep
On the edge of a wood our Will should sleep.
     God knows best!
But the years are long since the lads went west.

Dorothy Una Ratcliffe

Other mourners had nearly a decade to wait before they could attain some form of closure. On 24 July 1927, the Menin Gate, the great memorial to the Missing of the Ypres Salient, was finally unveiled in the presence of largely, but not exclusively, generals, diplomats, royalty and other worthies. This gate in Ypres was chosen, as the Commonwealth War Graves Commission explains, 'because of the hundreds of thousands of men who passed through it on their way to the battlefields'. The names carved on the panels of Portland Stone are those of circa 57,895 officers and men of this salient, whose bodies were either never found or could not be identified.

Amongst those who attended the unveiling were 700 pilgrims drawn from society's poorest bereaved, their presence paid for by the charitable St Barnabas Society. These contemporary bereaved who kissed or ran their fingers across their loved ones' names, and indeed the hundreds of thousands of pilgrims who have since gazed in awe at the names reaching up as far as the eye can see, may know the answer to the question VAD Carola Oman posed when, soon after the Armistice, she stood on the Menin Road.

THE MENIN ROAD, MARCH 1919

Over the flat dim land I see you moving
Methodically; under a dark wide sky
Full of low clouds. You are gone from our loving.
No fret of ours or grief can touch you now.
The road speaks nothing to our longing now.
The winds are dumb to us and pass us by.
The nameless tracks, the faded grass
Spread out as far as we can see.
The homeless shadows glance and pass
By shattered wood and naked tree.
Splintered and stark they rise alone
Against so wonderful a blue
Of distance – an intensity
At once so steadfast and so true.
I wonder are you wholly gone?

Carola Oman

Conclusion: 'Shall I ever forget you …?'

From the War's earliest days sorrows were given words. Words that still speak to us from a previous century, give a glimpse of how a generation ill-prepared for death and destruction on such a monumental scale found an outlet for grief in verse.

Some women, be they black-gowned or with faces falsely 'gay', gained solace from imagining their loved one's internment, surrounded by brothers-in-arms paying their dignified, final respects. Others accepted that, far from the comforting rites of the Anglican burial service, shell and shrapnel had been the audible backdrop to the Padre's hurried words.

A generation of parents found themselves awaiting an old age bereft of their beloved child and his progeny. Many mothers found comfort in retreating to precious memories of a son's boyhood, taking pride in his manly sacrifice. This helped to alleviate the inevitable guilt and grief at not having been with him when he died. Inexplicably, grief for sons was easily and widely poeticized, silence surrounds the mourning of those bereaved of a daughter or daughters.

Siblings' poetry shows how deeply many mourned their lost brothers or indeed their 'sisters-in-arms'. Sibling grief transcended generations, those approaching middle-age were robbed of the dearly-loved keeper of shared memories, whilst other women who now anticipated remaining single mourned the loss of unborn children.

Not all the bereaved had official status nor even the right to grieve openly. Poignant words hint at how disenfranchised mourners were excluded from the community, both real or imagined, of the bereaved. Many accepted their marginalization, others longed for recognition of their share in his memory.

Women's writings also give an insight into the anguish of sacrificing their sexual fulfilment. Contrary to contemporary mores, some women openly declared passionate, unashamed love, rejecting chaste idealization and celebrating, or at least dreaming of, intoxicating physical love. If all that remained were memories of shared passion, they would cling to these.

Throughout this long and bloody conflict, the bereaved sought many forms of comfort, some found this in actions, others in art, many in words. Some used conventional versification and High Diction to poeticize their resignation to the Divine Will, their belief in the chivalry of the modern Crusaders, their acceptance that, in wartime, women must weep. For others, these were merely outdated platitudes; they sought a poetic outlet for their grief, passion and anguish but nineteenth century poesy proved inadequate to these demands.

Traditionalist or modernist, these poems takes us to the heart of women's war, women's sacrifice, women's grief.

Conclusion:
'Whose the harder part?'

Writing in the *Daily Mail* on 24 September 1916, Galloway Kyle, Managing Director of Erskine Macdonald and Honorary Director of the Poetry Society, praised 'the rare quality and beauty of [women's] war verse'. He was far from alone in making such comments.

Fifteen years later, on 4 November 1933 the *Hastings and St Leonard Observer* reported how at a recent public lecture entitled 'Some Modern Women Poets', the speaker had argued convincingly that 'women poets were bound to look upon things from a different point of view but in sincerity, technique and beauty, the poems of women were not below those of men'. The lecturer singled out for praise a number of the 'war poetesses', tacitly recognising that although the shibboleth of sex had prevented women from bearing arms, that shibboleth had not prevented them from wielding their poetic pens.

Six days later, the *Derby Daily Telegraph* reported that speaking at Derby Guildhall, politician and lecturer on literature David Rennie Hardman had roundly refuted a claim made by the post-war generation of poets that Great War poetry had been 'purely sentimental'. He maintained that the Great War poets wrote 'from experience' and, as far as he was concerned, a woman's experience of wartime was as valid as a man's. These and many other critics, reviewers and lecturers both during and in the decades immediately following the War, accepted that irrespective of whether they were soldier or civilians, male or female, war poets were, from the outset, 'all in it together'.

But with the passing of time, the story of the Great European War for Civilisation became increasingly told – or listened to – through the voices of those dubbed 'soldier poets'. Those whose gender had made it possible for them to have been at the Front were increasingly automatically assumed to have been there. The term 'War Poet' became slowly and misleadingly synonymous with those presumed, rightly or wrongly, to have experienced front line action. The works of poets like Wilfred Gibson, who had rarely soldiered closer to a foreign field than Sydenham in Kent, appear in collections of poems penned by those deemed to have been 'up the line to death'.

Yet, poets such as Celia Congreve, who was within sight and sound of the guns from September 1914 to beyond the Armistice, were never included. If masculinity could blur the distinction between those who fought and those who did not, femininity worked the opposite way. The very fact of being female meant that a woman could not bear arms, ergo she was not a 'soldier poet'. Her poetry, or so this logic went, had nothing to say about war. Gradually, Great War poetry became a male preserve and the voices of women poets were silenced for decades.

The publication of Catherine Reilly's anthology *Scars Upon My Heart: Women's Poetry and Verse of the First World War* (1981), Nosheen Khan's critical appraisal *Women's Poetry of the First World War* (1988), the early 1990s work of feminist historians and my own PhD thesis *Songs of Wartime Lives: Women's Poetry of the First World War* (2004) alerted a new generation of critics to the existence of the considerable corpus of women's poetry. But these studies still barely lifted the curtain on the women's poetic war.

As stated in the Introduction, not all the poets who feature in this anthology were skilled – although a number were. The poems were chosen not on grounds of literary merit but to enhance and provide a different understanding of women's lives during those tumultuous years. Ranging from the confident, disturbing, modernist voice of Vassar-educated Mary Borden to the grief-stricken lines penned by bereaved mother and shipyard-labourer's widow Sarah Toye, these poems all tell a story.

Occasionally through dissenting voices, sometimes triumphalist and frequently despairing, women poets write of their gender's quiet heroism and steadfastness. They bring to agonising life the heart-stopping moment of bidding loved ones farewell and they tell of mundane tasks, such as knitting socks and queuing for food, as well as the dangers of making munitions. They transport us into the hospital wards and show the desolation of nursing the wounded. In a more religious age than our own, these Christian poets help us to understand their need to seek solace in religion. Uniformed poets speak of the camaraderie of women's service, allow us to empathise with the loneliness of tilling the land and to enter into the hard road back to 'Civvy Street'. Bereaved poets give us a glimpse into the heartbreak of war deaths and the lives of those who faced lonely, barren years ahead.

These poems speak to us across the century and enable us to listen to an alternative story of those fateful years. This is a story told through the quiet voices of those who, in S Gertrude Ford's words, were forced to learn the bitter lesson that whilst 'Men made the war; mere women' had to live through its terrible consequences.

Perhaps after reading this anthology you will find yourself, as I do, unable to answer the question Jessie Wakefield posed in the *Westminster Gazette* on 27 January 1915:

WHOSE?

The moment came. We said good-bye with smiles,
Sad smiles; each for the other's sake was brave.
Before you lay the perilous ocean miles,
The trenches and perhaps – who knows? – a grave.
I mourned my loneliness to come. "Dear heart"
You said, "Whose is the lonelier part?"

And now for me remains the shell of life;
A round of days that pass without a goal;
Dark, wakeful endless night with anguish rife,
When Fear long-chained, stalks forth and rules my soul.
Lover of mine afar or near, dear heart,
Say now; Whose is the harder part?

Jessie Wakefield

Whose, indeed?

Acknowledgements

Permission to reprint copyright poems in this book is gratefully acknowledged. Many holders have kindly waived a fee and a donation in recognition of their generosity has been made to the veterans' mental health charity Combat Stress (www.combatstress.org.uk) and Never Such Innocence (www.neversuchinnocence.com): Never Such Innocence is dedicated to educating young people about the First World War, its impact and legacy, through poetry, art and theatre. Apologies are offered to those copyright holders whom, despite every effort having been made, it has proved impossible to locate.

Poet, collection, title and publisher

Aldington, May, 'After', *Roll of Honour, and Other Poems*, Adams, 1917.

Allen, Marian, 'Charing Cross', *The Wind On The Downs, and Other Poems*, Humphreys, 1918.

Bagnold, Enid, 'The Guns of Kent', *The Sailing Ships*, Heinemann, 1918 (reprinted with permission of Dominick Jones).

Baker, Madeleine, Stuart, 'Autumn in England 1919', from *Collected Poems*, Mitre Press, 1961.

Bartlett, Brenda, 'Too Well', from *Songs of the Younger Born*, Erskine Macdonald, 1919.

Beatty, Mabel, 'The Walrus and the Carpenter', found in the papers of Violet Waldy in the Peter Liddle Archive, University of Leeds Brotherton Library (LIDDLE/WW1/WO/128).

Bedford, Madeleine, 'Munition Wages' from *The Young Captain, (and Other Poems): Fragments of War and Love*, Erskine Macdonald, 1917.

Betts Margery, 'Dead Men's Dreams' from *Remembering and other Verses*, Melbourne, 1917.

Bignold, Esther, Private poem.

Borden, Mary, 'Unidentified', 'At the Somme: The Song of the Mud', 'The Virgin of Albert' from *The Forbidden Zone*, Heinemann, 1929; 'No, no! There is some sinister mistake', reprinted with permission of Patrick Aylmer (Accessed 30 May 2015, via: www.allaboutheaven.org/

observations/11148/221/borden-mary-no-no-there-is-some-sinister-mistake-013106.

Boyle, Mary E, 'Sonnet V', *Aftermath*, Heffer, Cambridge 1916.

Braimbridge, Kathleen, 'Khaki Magic', *Dream-Songs (Poems)*, Elkin Matthews, 1916.

Bristowe, Sybil, 'My Garden', 'To His Dear Memory', *Provocations (Poems)*, Erskine Macdonald, 1918.

Bristles, 'Shanghai in June', *Old Comrades Association Gazette*, June 1923.

Brittain Vera, 'The German Ward', 'The Sisters Buried at Lemnos', *Verses of a VAD*, Erskine McDonald, 1918 (reprinted with permission of Mark Bostridge).

Burr, Amelia, 'The Woman at Home', *A Collection of Poems Relating To The European War 1914-1918 From Newspapers Magazines etc.*

Cannan, May Wedderburn, 'The Armistice. In an Office in Paris', *The Splendid Days*, Blackwell, 1919 (reprinted with permission of Mrs Clara Abrahams).

Charton, Miss, *My Lady's Garden*, Watts and Co., 1921.

Collins, Mary G, 'Women at Munition Making' from *Branches Unto The Sea (Poems)*, Erskine Macdonald, 1916.

Congreve, Celia, 'Lay Your head On The Earth's Breast' from *The Castle and Other Verses*, Humphreys, 1920.

Corrin, Theodora, 'Munitions Work: An Uncensored Letter' in *Lawrence Levy Donation Scrapbook II*, (Birmingham War Poetry Collection).

Coxford, Mrs., 'In Memoriam', *A Collection of Poems Relating To The European War 1914-1918 From Newspapers Magazines etc.*

Cranmer, Elsie P., 'Premonition', 'Maid Virtue', 'Remembrance', *To The Living Dead and Other Poems*, Daniel, 1920.

Cruttwell, Mary, 'Sunday Evening in a Public Park, 'Two Scarecrows in the Snow' *New Poems*, Morland, 1920.

Dircks, Helen, 'Munitions', *Finding and Other Poems*, Chatto&Windus, 1918.

Dobell, Eva, 'Pluck', 'Night Duty', *A Bunch of Cotswold Grasses (Poems)*, Stockwell, 1919.

Downes, Olive P, 'Friends Only' from *The Bridge of Memory (Poems)*, Stockwell, 1921.

Eden, Helen, Parry, 'Ars Immortalis' *Coal & Candlelight*, Bodley Head, 1918.

Eggleston Amy Untitled poem in ed. Harry Dounce *Sock Songs*, Cornhill, New York, 1919.

Elliot, Gabrielle, 'Pierrot Goes to War', G H Clarke ed. *A Treasury of War Poetry*, Houghton Mifflin Company, New York, 1919.

Falconer, Agnes, 'Scottish Nurses in Serbia', Graham, Peter A ed., *The Country Life Anthology*, Newnes, 1915.

Few, Marguerite, 'The Débutante 1917', *Laughing Gas and other poems*, Perkin Warbeck, Cambridge, 1921.

Florine, Margaret, 'To a Red Cross Nurse', *Songs of a Nurse*, Philopolis Press, California, 1918.

Ford, S Gertrude, 'War between Christians', *Poems of War and Peace*, Erskine Macdonald, 1915.

Ford, Vivien, 'The World's Chalice', *The Bookman*, October 1914.

Fuller-Maitland, Ella, 'Lines Written in Devon January 1915', *A Vision and Others 1915-1916*, Chiswick, 1916.

Furse, Margaret C, 'Captivity', *The Gift*, Constable, 1919.

Gibbons, Mary K, 'Time Will Win – Knit a Twin' in ed. Harry Dounce, *Sock Songs*.

Gillespie, Violet, 'Remembering' *Poems of 1915 and other Verse*, Erskine Macdonald 1915.

Glemby, Sophie, 'My Socks', Dounce ed. *Sock Songs*, Cornhill, New York, 1919.

Gotelee, K M E, 'To the Tune of Keep the Home Fires Burning', *The Landswoman*, April 1918.

Graham, Muriel, E, 'The Nameless Dead', *Vibrations and Others*, Erskine Macdonald, 1918.

Grantham, Alexandra, Sonnets XIX and XXI, *Mater Dolorosa*, Heinemann, 1915.

Grindlay, I, 'My Army Hat', 'To I. Cruden', 'Small Mercies', *Ripples from the Ranks of the QMAAC (Poems)*, Erskine Macdonald, 1918.

Grigsby, Joan, (See Rundall Joan).

Hamilton, Helen, 'The Retaliators', 'Prudes in a Fight', *Napoo! A Book of War Bêtes-Noires*, Blackwell, 1918.

Hamilton-Fellowes, Margery, 'An Evening Hymn in Time of War', *A Collection of Poems Relating To The European War 1914-1918 From Newspapers Magazines etc.*

Harris, Ada, 'Red Cross Car' in *A Collection of Poems Relating To The European War 1914-1918 From Newspapers Magazines etc.*

Henderson, Mary, 'An Incident', 'In Memoriam Elsie Maud Inglis', 'Like That', *In War and Peace: Songs of A Scotswoman*, Erskine Macdonald, 1918.

Hinkson, Pamela, 'A Song of Autumn', *A Collection of Poems Relating To The European War 1914-1918 From Newspapers Magazines etc.*

Jenkins, Elinor, 'The Last Evening', 'Ecce Homo', *Poems; Last Poems*, Sidgwick, 1921.

Jeffrey, Mabel, 'In Memoriam', *Auntie Mabel's War: An Account of Her Part in the Hostilities of 1914-18*, compiled by Marian Wenzel and John Cornish, Allen Lane, 1980.

Key, Helen, 'Edith Cavell', *Broken Music (Poems)*, Elkin Matthew, 1916.

Letts, Winifred, M, 'The Call to Arms in Our Street', 'A Sister in a Military Hospital', 'Heart's Desire', 'July 1916', *The Spires of Oxford*, Dutton, New York, 1917.

Lindsay, Lady Kathleen, 'Munitions Alphabet' found in the papers of Lady Kathleen Lindsay in the Peter Liddle Archive, University of Leeds Brotherton Library, (LIDDLE/WW1/DF/076).

Mackay, Helen, 'Train', 'Park', 'The Courtesan', *London One November*, Andrew Melrose, 1915.

Maitland, Ella Fuller (See Fuller-Maitland).

Mansfield, Katherine, 'To L.H.B. 1894-1915', *Poems*, Constable, 1923.

Mardel, Nina, 'I Shall Never Feel' from *Plain Song (Poems)*, Erskine Macdonald, 1917.

Maynard, Constance, 'Watching the War' and 'Mourning in Berlin', *Watching The War*, Allenson, 1914.

Mayor, Beatrice, 'Spring 1917', *Poems*, Allen & Unwin, 1919 (reprinted with permission of David Mayor and Victoria Gray).

Meynell, Alice, 'Summer in England 1914' from *A Father of Women and other poems*, Burns & Oates, 1917.

Murray, E M, *Old Comrades Association Newsletter No. 3. 1937.*

Oman, Carola, 'The Menin Road March 1919', *The Menin Road*, Hodder &Stoughton, 1919. (reprinted with permission of Sir Roy Strong).

Orr, Emily, 'A Recruit from the Slums', *A Harvester of Dreams*, Burnes, Oates & Washbourne, 1922.

Parker, Mrs, 'The Convert' in *The Bookman*, October 1915.

Pope, Jessie, 'Socks' from *War Poems*, Grant Richards, 1915.

Ratcliffe, Dorothy, Una, 'Remembrance Day in the Dales' *Singing Rivers (Poems)*, Bodley Head, 1922.

Renshaw, Constance, 'The Lure of England', *England's Boys*, Erskine Macdonald, 1916.

Rundall, Joan, 'The Farm of the Apple Tree', *Peatsmoke and Other Verses*, H F W Deane, 1919.

Sackville, Margaret, 'Sacrament', 'Victory', 'The Dead', *Collected Poems*, Martin Secker, 1939.

Scheffauer, Ethel Talbot, 'Spiders', 'Easter 1918', *New Altars*, William Kupe, Berlin, 1921.

Scott, Aimée Byng, 'The Farewell', *The Road to Calais and other poems*, Thacker, 1919.

Sinclair, May, 'To A Field Ambulance in Flanders', *Journal of Impressions in Belgium*, Hutchinson, 1915; 'After The Retreat', *The Egoist* 1 May 1915.

Smyth, Marjorie Kane 'Armistice Day' *Poems*, Morland Foyle, Amersham, 1919.

Spender, Violet, 'In Memoriam A.F.S.', *The Path to Spender and other poems*, Sidgwick and Jackson, 1922.

Stone, M, 'The Hoarder'; 'Kent 'A' Garden', *Women's Volunteer Reserve*, Magazine 1916-1919.

Stuart, Muriel, 'Forgotten Dead, I Salute You', *Poems*, Heinemann, 1922, (reprinted with permission of John Stapleforth).

Teasdale, Sara, 'Spring in War-Time', J W Cunliffe ed., *Poems of the Great War*, Macmillan Company, New York, 1916.

Tollemache, Evelyn, 'The Leave Train Victoria Station', *The New Crucifixion and Other Poems*, Stockwell, 1918.

Toye, Sarah, 'In Memory of Private John Vincent', Private poem, (reprinted with permission of Roz Luftus).

Caroline A L Travers, 'May 1915', *A Pocketful of Rye*, privately printed Martin and Sturt, Farnham c.1916.

Trotter, Alys, F, 'Picardie', (Accessed August 2014 ua: www.indymedia.org. uk/en/2012/11/502521.htm); 'Summer 1917', *Nigel & Other Verses*, Burns & Oates, 1918.

Tynan, Katharine, 'Joining the Colours', *Flower of Youth*, Sidgwick & Jackson, 1915.

Tyrrell-Green, Margaret, 'I Will a Tomb Upraise', *More Poems*, Arrowsmith, Bristol, 1918.

Verne, Viviane, 'Kensington Gardens', *A Casket of Thoughts (Poems)*, Simkin Marshall Hamilton, 1916.

Vickridge, Alberta, 'The Red Cross Sister', *The Sea Gazer and Other Poems*, Erskine Macdonald, 1919.

Wallace, Kathleen M, 'Because You Are Dead', *Lost City: Verses*, Heffer, Cambridge, 1918.

Wedgwood, Winifred, M, 'Our VAD Scullions', *Verses of A VAD Kitchen-Maid*, Gregory & Scott, Torquay, 1917.

Whitmell, Lucy, 'Christ in Flanders', Frederick Brereton ed., *An Anthology of War Poems*, William Collins and Co., 1930.

Appendix 1

Biographies of the Poets

JESSIE MAY ALDINGTON (1873-1954)

A somewhat sensational novelist, Jessie May Aldington came from a less socially privileged background than her solicitor husband. The family fell on hard financial times, leading their son Edward (who later changed his name to Richard) to cease his studies at the University of London. He enlisted in 1916; in addition to being severely gassed on the Western Front, Richard almost certainly suffered from shell-shock. His 1929 novel, *Death of a Hero*, is considered at least partly autobiographical, although whether the description of the narrator's mother having a number of lovers is based on May is hard to ascertain.

MARIAN ALLEN (1892-1953)

Australian-born Marian Allen lived in Oxford for several years before the War. In 1913, her brother had introduced her to his friend and fellow Law student, Arthur Tylston Greg. The two young men joined up in the 1914 wave of enthusiasm. In his letters home throughout 1915, Arthur mentioned the sister of a university friend, who 'writes me such interesting letters' and who 'sent me the Easter eggs'.

Wounded initially in December 1914, part of Arthur's jaw was then shot away at Ypres in May 1915. After a lengthy recovery, he followed Marian's brother into the Royal Flying Corps in September 1916. By December 1916, he had completed a training course with the Royal Naval Air Service. When he achieved his aviator's certificate in January 1917, he had clocked up twenty-seven hours' practice. On 4 April 1917, he and Marian said what would be their final farewell at London's Charing Cross Station.

Posted to 55 Squadron, where the life expectancy of newly arrived pilots was under a fortnight, Arthur took part in a St George's Day bombing raid; he and his observer were shot down and killed. Marian received news of Arthur's death the following week, no doubt via either his parents or her brother. As a fiancée she would have had no official status in his life and news of his welfare had to filter through via the next-of-kin. This situation left many young women wondering, sometimes for significant lengths of time, what had happened to their beloved. More than one woman admits in poetry, diaries or memoirs that she had been desperate to marry 'her' serviceman in order to be sure that she would be the first to know if the worst happened.

Marian's autobiographical series of sonnets, *The Wind on the Downs*, is dedicated to 'A.T.G.' His train ticket, number 7935, remained one of her most treasured possessions until she died, unmarried, in September 1953.

ENID BAGNOLD (1890-1981)

Born in Rochester, Kent, the daughter of a colonel in the Royal Engineers, Enid spent part of her childhood in Jamaica but was educated in Surrey. She was eager to break away from the stultifying chaperoned atmosphere of pre-1914 England and, rather shockingly for the time, took a flat in Chelsea, studied Art, and in 1913 became a staff writer on a new magazine, *Modern Society*.

Enid enrolled as a VAD and in 1917 she achieved brief wartime notoriety with her controversial account of hospital life, *Diary without Dates*. This led to her instant dismissal. She subsequently went to France as an ambulance driver with the FANY and based her semi-autobiographical novel *The Happy Foreigner* (1920) on her experiences. Less controversial was her 1918 poetry collection *The Sailing Ships*. 'The Guns of Kent', which first appeared in *The Nation* on 20 July 1918, was addressed to Siegfried Sassoon, whom Bagnold rightly felt was unjustified in his scathing condemnation of women.

Bagnold later achieved considerable fame as an author, her most famous novel being *National Velvet*.

MADELEINE STUART BAKER (1882-1962)

Madeleine and her sister Lily were amongst the earliest Irish female doctors, achieving MB (Bachelor of Medicine) degrees from Trinity College Dublin in 1907. In 1910, Baker became the first woman to be awarded an MD (Doctor of Medicine) by Trinity College Dublin. She later worked near Somerset as a medical practitioner and tuberculosis physician. During the First World War, Madeleine became an Honorary Major in the RAF medical service, whilst her sister followed a distinguished career as an obstetrician in Bath – the first female doctor to be appointed as a full member of staff in a British hospital outside London.

MABEL BEATTY (1880-1932)

Born in Sussex, Mabel married a Civil Service solicitor. Between 1916 and 1918, she sought to organize all women's voluntary work under a general 'Green Cross Society' or Women's Ambulance Reserve. These uniformed women filled multiple roles, ranging from driving ambulances (they were the first on the scene following the first major Zeppelin raid on London in September 1915), serving as housemaids and orderlies in hospitals and military clubs, working in hospital supply depots, to running night-time canteens for munitions workers.

Mabel may have feared that the creation of a Woman's Royal Naval Service would suck volunteers away from her own endeavours. A forceful advocate of women's uniformed service, she was empathetic towards working-class women who were seizing the more highly paid job opportunities that the War offered, but she was scathing towards the affluent 'idle woman' who did not volunteer her services.

On 7 June 1918, Mabel Beatty was gazetted CBE for her work as Commandant of the Green Cross Society.

MADELINE BEDFORD (1884-1956)

Born in Woolwich, Madeline's civil engineer father undoubtedly worked at the Royal Arsenal. In 1911, the family was living in Erith close to Woolwich Arsenal, an important wartime munitions making area.

It is possible that she too worked at the Arsenal, perhaps as a 'lady volunteer', as the middle-class women who worked for free in the factories were called. Either way, living so close to the Arsenal meant that she would have seen and heard workers thronging through the factory gates at the beginning and end of shifts and heard their 'devil-may-care' talk. Factory black humour was similar to that of the trenches.

Madeline dedicated her poetry collection, *The Young Captain*, 'To the radiant and beautiful memory of my beloved and only brother Terence KIA France May 28th 1917'.

MARGERY RUTH BETTS (1892-1981)

Born in England, Margery was the daughter of a Congregational Minister. By 1914 she was living in Victoria, Australia and her wartime poems appeared in Australian newspapers. After spending time in England in 1920 as a student, she returned to Australia.

One poem from her collection, *Remembering* (1917), was used in Australian schools at the end of the War. Her poetry was also published in local English papers and it appealed sufficiently to one officer for him to send a selection to his local newspaper *The Cornishman*. The reviewer felt that her poetry would 'live in memory when peace returned to the world'.

ESTHER BIGNOLD (1855-1921)

The daughter of a grocer and pork butcher, in 1876 Esther married umbrella manufacturer Alfred Bignold. This poem was written for the youngest of her twelve children, Grace, who joined the Red Cross in May 1915.

By April 1919, 21-year-old Grace had clocked up some 5,000 hours as a VAD in several hospitals, before transferring to Streatham Auxiliary Red Cross [Convalescent] Hospital. In 1916 the hospital had thirty-three beds, three trained nurses (subsequently reduced to two), three full-time, and fourteen part-time local VADs. Impressively, only one patient of the total 930 admissions died. Grace's 'own soldier', farrier Frederick Francke, enlisted in 1914 and rose to the rank of Acting Warrant Officer, ending his military career as a cyclist with the Royal Fusiliers. They married in 1921; Grace died in 1983.

MARY BORDEN (1886-1968)

One of the War's finest poets, Vassar-educated Mary Borden was the daughter of a Chicago millionaire father and Christian fundamentalist mother. Pregnant when war was declared, she gave her name to the London Committee of the French Red Cross, declaring her willingness to become a volunteer nurse, despite having no nursing skills and only a basic knowledge of French.

In January 1915, recently delivered of her third daughter, Mary went to Malo-les-Bains, where she became an excellent nurse. Fired up with enthusiasm, in July 1915 she financed her own Unit, Hôpital Chirurgical Mobile No 1, yet she came to learn from bitter experience that, despite personnels' best efforts, medical ministrations were often futile, nurses were unable to cope with what she referred to as the 'effluvia of mud, dirt, blood'. Her war service led to the break-up of her already faltering first marriage and her subsequent marriage to Captain Edward Louis Spears – whose first glimpse of her was, as her sonnet declares, in her 'mud-splattered and blood-stained apron' in summer 1916.

Borden's masterpiece, *The Forbidden Zone*, graphically recounts in prose and poetry the conditions in which she and her volunteer nurses worked when stationed near Bray-sur-Somme – an important supply dump for munitions and other army equipment during the build-up to and throughout the Battle of the Somme. They were frequently within earshot of the guns and saw men staggering back from the battlefields as well as, in September 1916, the very first tanks to be used in battle trundling down the road.

Considered too graphic by the censors, *The Forbidden Zone* was not published until 1929, although her poetry appeared in periodicals, particularly *The English Review*, from 1917. In her writing, Borden doubts whether the blood spilled with such profligacy could redeem the world. In her view a man's life-blood was oozing away, not a convenient poetic symbol to mask reality and elevate dying soldiers into modern Lambs of God.

MARY E BOYLE (1882-1951)

Daughter of Rear-Admiral Robert Boyle, Mary was born in Renfrewshire, Scotland. She was very close to her youngest brother, David, eight years her junior, who became a career soldier and served with the 2nd Battalion, the Lancashire Fusiliers. One of the War's earliest casualties, David was killed on 26 August 1914 at Le Cateau – his body was never found.

Each of the thirty sonnets (the poetic form chosen because this was apparently David's favourite) Mary composed for him and published in *Aftermath*, focuses on some aspect of their shared past, although she recognises that as he grew to manhood their paths diverged. Her other brother, Archibald, survived the War, having won two Military Crosses. As Air-Commodore Boyle, he became the SOE's Director of Security in World War Two. Mary and her sister do not appear in the 1901 census. Her sister married in India so it is possible that Mary spent some time there. In 1926, when travelling to the USA, Mary gave her occupation as 'lecturer' and she crossed the Atlantic extensively.

Scottish poet and critic Hugh McDiarmid considered her 1922 children's collection, *Daisies and Apple Trees*, 'delightful'. Mary Boyle also translated works from French and wrote widely on pre-history. In 1937, she was elected Fellow of the Society of Antiquaries.

KATHLEEN BRAIMBRIDGE (1884-1949)

A native of Kidderminster, Kathleen was educated at Milton Mount College, Gravesend, a school that catered primarily for girls who were Congregational ministers' daughters. According to research carried out by North Kent Archaeological Society, on 4 June 1915 a bomb dropped near this school, shattering several windows. The girls subsequently slept on the ground floor with respirators and necessary clothes nearby. Three weeks later, the school was closed (reopening the following term in Cirencester).

In 1918, the Admiralty briefly requisitioned the impressive College buildings to serve as a venereal disease hospital. At the time this was considered to besmirch the school's reputation, making it impossible for the girls and their female teachers to return there. Hospitals for sexually transmitted diseases were essential nonetheless – just under 417,000 men were hospitalised for this reason – exceeding the numbers admitted with trench foot.

The 24 August 1917, the *Royal Leamington Spa Courier and Warwickshire Gazette* poetry reviewer praised Kathleen's 'Khaki Magic', feeling it struck a chord with Kidderminster residents due to the number of weaving factories in the town.

SYBIL BRISTOWE (1871–1954)

One of ten children born to a physician, Sybil's younger brother, 42-year-old Vivian, served with the South Africa Medical Corps, dying of dysentery in Tanzania in 1917. It is hard to know what led Vivian, a member of the Stock Exchange, to serve and die so far from home, although there are poetic hints in *Provocations* that Sybil and perhaps her brother had spent time in South Africa. Some of her war poems appeared in the *Johannesburg Star*.

Sybil was an enthusiastic gardener, whilst acknowledging that a garden in London's Maida Vale was not the easiest place in which to grow flowers – or vegetables.

VERA BRITTAIN (1893–1970)

Perhaps the best known female poet of the First World War, Vera Brittain was the daughter of a paper mill owner. In 1911, the Brittain family were living in Buxton, Derbyshire. Vera's brother, Edward enlisted against his father's wishes in September 1914 and by October 1914, she too had overcome parental opposition and entered Somerville College, Oxford, to read English Literature.

Before the War, Vera had formed an attachment to her brother's friend Roland Leighton. In 1915, she left Oxford, determined to assist the war effort. Arguably the War's most famous VAD, *Testament of Youth* (1933) is based on her war diaries and her experiences in England and overseas. The loss of Roland, her closest friends and her brother epitomised many women's traumatic war losses and remains a well-loved text to this day, having been made into a film released in 2015.

Vera returned to Somerville in 1918 to study History, in an attempt to understand what had catapulted the world into a war of such magnitude and devastating consequences. She struggled to re-adapt to university life, surrounded by undergraduates too young to have experienced or even to empathise with the full horrors and grief she had undergon. *Verses of a VAD* (1918) is based on her experiences in the wards.

AMELIA BURR (1878-1968)

Born and educated in New York, Amelia worked for the American Red Cross in 1917-18. After the War, she married a clergyman. Her patriotic, jingoistic poetry found great favour with the Vigilantes, an American organisation formed in March 1917 and designated as an auxiliary to the Bureau of Investigation of the Department of Justice. Their pamphlets and newspapers were distributed with the intention of inspiring patriotism and Allied involvement in the War.

One of the Vigilantes' aims was to distribute patriotic poetry to newspapers – American papers being as eager to publish poetry as British ones. As well as featuring in Vigilantes' anthologies, Burr published four volumes of war poetry and numerous newspaper poems. Childless herself, she frequently blames women, especially mothers, for men's failure to enlist. She was equally quick to chastise those who, with no son to give, were slow to invest in War Bonds.

MAY WEDDERBURN CANNAN (1893-1973)

May was the second daughter of an Oxford dean, who was in charge of the Oxford University Press between 1895 and 1919. Before the War she had taken Red Cross nursing certificates and she became VAD Quartermaster in Oxford.

May's autobiography, *Grey Ghosts and Voices* (1976), gives a moving account of her war culminating in her anguish at the death of her fiancé, Bevil Quiller-Couch, from Spanish 'flu in early 1919. He had refrained from proposing to her until the end of the War, when he felt that there was a strong possibility that he would survive long enough for them to marry – which they planned to do in June 1919. The intensely personal poetry she wrote following his death gives an intimate glimpse into female bereavement. She did eventually marry and her husband, Percival James Slater, a balloonist in the First World War, became a brigadier in the Second. Her work is frequently anthologised.

CAROLINE A L TRAVERS (CALT) (1873-1958)

Caroline Travers was the wife of an employee of the London Colonial Service, who served as a much loved and respected doctor and surgeon for many years in Kuala Lumpur – having been a ship's surgeon by the age of twenty-two. She consistently gives her occupation as 'housewife'. The couple returned to

Malaysia after the War. Caroline appears to have travelled extensively post-war. She had poems published in *The Englishwoman* and this allows us to assume that she was well-educated and had at least an interest in women's suffrage.

MISS CHARTON

No information located apart from the suggestion in her published volumes that she had a London home near Chelsea Barracks and also spent time in Sussex. Her two book-length poems, *Hackleplume* and *My Lady's Garden*, are amongst the War's most unusual works.

'BEATRICE CHASE' (1874-1955)

'Beatrice Chase' was the pen name of Olive Katherine Parr. Henry VIII's sixth and final queen was her many times great-aunt. She lived from the turn of the century in Dartmoor and this location informed much of her fiction. Highly eccentric, Olive fought vigorously to protect Dartmoor from developers as well as against its use by the British Army.

A devout Catholic, she also campaigned for both male and female purity. According to her *Who's Who* entry, she was Foundress of the Crusade of White Knights and Ladies and 'sole organiser of the Crusade for Chastity, which numbers among its members some of the most distinguished civilians, clergy, and officers in the Empire'. Whether she kept her promise to write letters to all who signed her purity charter is unknown, as is the number of signatories. Shortly before her death Olive was considered by her local health authority to be a person 'in need of care and attention'. It would appear that she disagreed with this verdict, as, according to local gossip, she was taken to hospital in a straitjacket, but only after the loaded revolver she kept by her bed had been removed. As she lived in a remote part of Dartmoor, she may have felt that the revolver provided her with some protection.

FLORENCE VAN CLEVE (1867-1946)

An American schoolmaster's wife, Florence may also have been a member of the Vigilantes group. She had many poems published in American newspapers throughout the war years showing sympathy with America's entry into the War and she also wrote lyrics for patriotic songs. According to the US census of 1930, Florence's husband and one of her twin sons served with the US forces, but no further information about their military records has been found.

Post-war she wrote some political poetry, including poems on the issue of unemployment.

MARY GABRIELLE COLLINS (1874–1945)

The eldest of eight children, Mary was born in Penderyn, Wales. In 1911, she was living in Golders Green, where she was employed as a journalist and acting as News Editor on a now unidentifiable 'Religious Weekly Newspaper'. 'Women at Munition Making' is the best known and most widely quoted poem from her collection *Branches Unto the Sea* (1916). Religious faith and despair at the horrors of war vie for poetic space in this volume. By 1927, the now Reverend Mary Collins was, most unusually for the time, a minister at the North Bow Congregational Church, 522 Old Ford Road, E8.

CELIA CONGREVE (1867–1952)

Celia was born in India to a regular officer in the Indian Army, whose name was put forward for the Victoria Cross (VC) for gallantry during the Indian Mutiny. In 1890, she married Lieutenant Walter Congreve, who won the VC at the 1899 Battle of Colenso. His recently discovered Christmas 1914 letter to Celia provides insight into the famous Christmas Truce, which he witnessed at Neuve-Chapelle.

Her eldest son, 25-year-old Brevet Major William, already gazetted MC and DSO, French Légion d'Honneur, gained a posthumous VC following his death on 20 July 1916, during the Battle of the Somme. He had been married some six weeks at the time.

Celia served with the Red Cross as a driver and nurse in Belgium and France from 1914. As well as War and Victory medals, she was awarded the Mons Star, the Medal of Queen Elizabeth of the Belgians, the Médaille de la Reconnaissance Française and, unusually for a woman, the French Croix de Guerre. Her younger son Geoffrey won the DSO in 1940 and was killed in 1941.

THEODORA CORRIN

No information has been found.

JANE (CLISH) COXFORD 1872–1941

Her coal miner husband died when she was in her early 20s. She re-married a coal mine hewer 8 years her junior in 1897. Her son, Harry, served with the

Yorkshire Hussars (Alexandra, Princess of Wales's Own); 19-year-old Harry died of wounds in November 1915. He is buried in Lijssenthoek Military Cemetery, the second largest Commonwealth War Graves Commission cemetery in Belgium, which served many of the CCS. A career soldier, Harry was on the Western Front by November 1914.

ELSIE PATERSON CRANMER (1896-1978)

By 1911, architect's daughter Elsie was a 'musical student'. She experienced multiple bereavements during the First World War. In September 1916 her brother, Rifleman Arthur Brede, was killed in France and in December 1916, another brother, Charles, died of wounds in England.

On 17 September 1917, Elsie Brede and Guy Paterson Cranmer 'former schoolmaster now serving with HM Forces', obtained a 'Special Licence' allowing them to marry on 23 September – there was insufficient time before Guy's return to the Front to call the banns. Guy was killed on 9 October. In late November 1917, her sister's fiancé, Machine Gunner Lieutenant Harold Rowbotham, a 25-year-old artist, was killed.

Elsie did not re-marry and may have earned her living, or supplemented her Army widow's pension, by writing and composing songs.

MARTHA FOOTE CROW (1854-1924)

Born in New York State to a clergyman father, Martha played a key role in developing higher education for women, at one point co-ordinating a survey of women's international higher education. Educated at Syracuse University, she was awarded a PhD in English literature in 1886. Married to the Principal of Iowa College, she became 'Lady Principal' of that establishment. As well as furthering the cause of women's university education, she was active in a number of literary and poetry societies.

EDITH MARY CRUTTWELL (1886-1968)

Daughter of a Norfolk clergyman, Edith published one volume of war poetry, *New Poems* (1920), and was also anthologised in Charles Forshaw's *One Hundred Best Poems of the European War by Women Poets of the Empire* (1916). Living in Bath in 1930, she gave her profession as 'artist' and her marital status as 'single' on a passenger list of travellers sailing to Gibraltar.

HELEN DIRCKS (1897–?)

Helen's father worked in publishing. As there were several munitions factories near her home in Middlesex, 'Munitions' may be based upon her own or at least observed experiences. She married novelist Frank Swinnerton in 1920, divorcing in 1924.

From the tone of a number of her poems in *Finding* (1918) and *Passenger* (1920), writing poetry was probably a form of grief work for a dead boyfriend or fiancé. In its 23 June 1920 edition, the *Spectator* considered Helen's work 'worthy of consideration'. She also wrote lyrics used in productions by Fred Karno, the famous Music Hall impresario. In 1935, she shocked fellow diners in a restaurant when she called for, lit, and smoked a cigar.

EVA DOBELL (1876–1963)

The daughter of a wine merchant, Eva was also the niece of Victorian poet Sydney Dobell. She served as a Nursing VAD at the Priory VA Hospital, Cheltenham from its opening day, 5 November 1914 to 11 November 1917. She nursed for thirty-six hours a week on a fully voluntary basis and also wrote to prisoners of war. This auxiliary hospital, which was unusual as it had both officers' and other ranks' wards, moved twice in order to accommodate increasing patient numbers. By the time it closed on 9 January 1919 there had been 1,603 admissions and 20 deaths; the average length of stay exceeded six weeks.

One poem from Eva's series 'In a Soldier's Hospital' was set to music. After the War she continued to write and also edited Lady Margaret Sackville's poetry.

OLIVE PRIMROSE DOWNES (1886–1927)

Born in Walthamstow, Olive was a solicitor's daughter and, although she had had a children's story published in 1909, the 1911 census gives her occupation as 'Nil'. Like many unmarried women of her age, Olive continued to reside with her parents during her adult life. She worked as a VAD during the First World War and in 1916 was at the well-equipped 85-bed Southall Auxiliary (Military Convalescent) Hospital. Some of her poems were published in *Herald of the Star*, the leading magazine of the organization The Order of the Star in the East to which a number of high profile individuals contributed.

The Order was an international theosophical organization founded to prepare the world for a new messianic [non-Christian] coming or World

Teacher. Lady Emily Lutyens was closely involved with it. Her husband, Edwin Lutyens was one of the principal architects involved with the creation of the Imperial War Graves (now Commonwealth) cemeteries, including the Memorial to the Missing of the Somme, as well as the architect of Viceroy House and many other key buildings in New Delhi and London.

HELEN PARRY EDEN (1885-1960)

Daughter of a judge, Helen was born in London and educated at Roedean School, Manchester University, and King's College Art School. She married painter William Denis Eden in 1907. Their daughter Betsey Anne features in several of her poems. Her poetry appeared in *Punch*, *Pall Mall Magazine*, *Catholic Messenger* and several wartime anthologies. Post-war, she continued to write religious texts and also published poetry in World War Two.

AMY EGGLESTON (1874-1929)

A frequent winner of *The New York Sun*'s knitting poems competition, Amy continued to write prize-winning poems which were published in newspapers until her death. Though childless herself, she was a prolific knitter and writer of knitting poems, empathizing with women whose heart missed a beat with every unexpected knock on the door.

GABRIELLE ELLIOT (1890-1988)

Born in New York, Gabrielle was educated at New York's prestigious women-only college, Vassar, founded in 1865 to provide an academically challenging education to women. Entrants had to know Latin, speak at least one foreign language and be well versed in both the Arts and the Sciences. On one occasion Gabrielle translated a play by seventeenth century French dramatist Molière, which was performed by the theatrical association.

Vassar had a reputation for producing strong, independently-minded graduates who set themselves and achieved high goals. Elliott's family had connections with France; her uncle, an expert pianist and organist played for the American Church in Paris. In August 1913, she and her mother visited Paris and she was later involved with two American charities supporting French soldiers and refugees.

Partly in acknowledgement of France's support of the USA's War of Independence, many Americans felt a debt of gratitude towards the country. In 1914, American women living abroad founded the American Fund for

French Wounded (AFFW), which aimed to provide much needed relief to small hospitals in France and medical assistance for wounded French soldiers and civilians. The charity also offered various forms of support for refugees, including those evacuated either by the Germans from their homes in Occupied France or by the French authorities in militarised zones.

The AFFW worked closely with the American Committee for Devastated France and the American Red Cross. Poems and indeed whole collections written by men and women from across the combatant nations were often sold to raise funds for local, national and international charities. It is likely that there was a fund-raising element to Elliot's poetry due to the extent of her charitable involvement.

Elliot was also involved with the Council of National Defense, which on April 21, 1917 (fifteen days after the USA's entry into the War), put out a statement targeting 'the women of America [who] may be made available in the prosecution of the war.' Perhaps learning from the experience of now war-hardened nations, the US Government immediately recognized the value of women's war work – although uncertainty surrounded what that should be.

AGNES S FALCONER (1869-1951)

Born in Scotland, Agnes's father was an ironmonger. Like a number of poets, she responded poetically to the September 1914 German burning of the Belgian town of Louvain and its cultural treasures. One unusual poem extols the benefits of 'Sphagnum Moss', which was widely used in the treatment of wounds; Scotland supplied many kilos of it. An active member of the Scottish Women's Rural Institute, Agnes' interests and sympathies lay with Scotland's rural communities. Despite damning her with relatively faint praise as a 'competent versifier', Scottish poet Hugh McDiarmid considered her a contributor to the Scottish Renaissance in poetry

The 'Sisters' she commemorates in the poem are Augusta Minshull, Madge Fraser and Louisa Jordan, who all died of typhus in Serbia within weeks of each other in March and April 1915, and Bessie Sutherland in September 1915. The atrocious conditions in Serbia were an ideal breeding-ground for the body lice that spread this highly contagious cold-weather disease. Dr Elizabeth Ross was the first of the British to succumb in February 1915, followed shortly by the nurses.

Serbia still honours the memories of the British women who gave their lives to their cause. Despite the best efforts of many hundreds of British doctors and nurses, they and the Serbian medical services fought a losing battle against horrific wounds, disease and vermin.

ELEANOR FARJEON (1881-1965) [Poem 'The Outlet' not quoted here, due to copyright issues]

Eleanor's novelist father encouraged his shy, bookish daughter to write from an early age. Awkward as a young woman, she met poet Edward Thomas in 1913 and formed a close friendship with him and his family. On learning of Thomas's death, his wife Helen immediately telegrammed Eleanor who rushed to the family's Epping Forest home to share their grief. She put her own mourning aside whilst she sought to comfort Helen, only returning to her own home several weeks after Edward's death. She recounts this in her poem 'The Outlet'.

In her deeply moving elegiac sonnets to Edward Thomas, Eleanor acknowledges her love for him and accepts that to Edward she was most probably little more than a dear, reliable friend with whom he had a close meeting of minds. However, one sonnet published long after the War hints that perhaps his feelings went deeper than friendship. Her *Edward Thomas The Last Four Years* reveals as much about her as about Thomas. In this, she demonstrates that she believed (as generations of scholars and Thomas aficionados have since) that, in Helen's words, 'his beloved body was not injured'.

Thomas' biographer Jean Moorcroft Wilson, has recently found evidence that he was 'shot clean through the chest' and this, rather than a shell blast causing his heart to stop, killed him. There is nothing unusual about Helen and Eleanor's need to believe that Edward's body was not mutilated – those who cannot see the body of their loved one often need to cling to the idea that it was perfect in death.

Eleanor's hymn 'Morning Has Broken' is still widely sung; it was recorded by the singer Cat Stevens. She never married, but in 1919 formed a thirty-year friendship with English teacher George Earle and, following his death, with the actor Denys Blakelock.

A prolific author of works for both adults and children, she is recognised as pivotal in the development of children's literature. The Children's Book Circle established the Eleanor Farjeon Award in her honour. She declined to become a Dame of the British Empire, not wishing 'to become different from the milkman.'

MAGUERITE FEW

No information has been uncovered about this poet. Her patriotic poetry appeared in local newspapers as well as the *Westminster Gazette*. She also had a collection, *Laughing Gas*, published in 1921.

MARGARET HELEN FLORINE (1880-1949)

Like so many women, professional nurse Margaret Florine has escaped critical notice. A brief review of her *Songs of a Nurse* appeared in the *San Francisco Chronicle* (7 October 1917) and the second edition was well reviewed in *American Journal of Nursing* (5 February 1920). The reviewer felt that the poems 'showed a rare sympathy and deep understanding of the thoughts and feelings of the many and varied broken beings brought to the hospital for repair.' Intriguingly, in the 1920 American census, she gives her father's place of birth as Germany but in the 1900 census it appears as France.

SOPHIA <u>GERTRUDE</u> FORD (1877-1947)

The daughter of a 'Church Chapel Keeper', Lancashire-born telephone operator and subsequently journalist Ford was a pacifist and feminist as well as a prolific poet. Several of her poems explore the irony of Christians fighting each other in this ghastly war, both sides convinced that right was on their side. Individual poems by Ford were widely published in pacifist-leaning papers. Profits from the sale of at least some of her work were donated to the British Red Cross Society.

VIVIEN FORD (1890-?)

Bristol-born Vivien Ford's father was a sufficiently prosperous corn merchant for his daughter not to need to work; she gives 'No Occupation' in the 1911 census. She had attended Clifton High School for Girls and seems to have retained links with the school, writing plays for post-war charitable productions put on by the 'Old Girls'. In 1916, one of Vivien's brothers was conscripted into the Army Pay Corps.

She won several of the many poetry competitions proposed in *The Bookman* from the War's earliest days. Her first success came in October 1914 with the award of one guinea (worth approximately £100 in 2016) for the 'the best original lyric'. She apparently had artistic as well as musical talent, as frequent mention is made of her musical contribution to Bristol cultural events in local papers.

MARGARET <u>CELIA</u> FURSE (1890-1975)

Daughter of Sir Henry Newbolt, the composer of the famous 1897 poem 'Vitai Lampada', throughout her childhood, Margaret was surrounded by the literati of the era. Sir Henry Newbolt was a member of the government initiated War

Propaganda Bureau, formed in September 1914 to guide public opinion in supporting the War. He did not approve of education for women, considering the home schoolroom and governesses ample for a woman's intellectual needs. His private life was more colourful than his public one, however, and his marriage consisted of a *ménage à trois* with his wife and her lesbian lover, who also became Newbolt's mistress. Though aware of these unusual domestic arrangements, Celia's affection for her father was undimmed.

In June 1914, she married Ralph Furse whose aunt, Katherine Furse, became Commandant of the VADs overseas and subsequently of the WRNS. According to an August 1910 letter, Ralph was 'a lively youth of remarkable looks who, when in a festive mood, liked to swish the heads off poppies with his sword'. Celia announced her first pregnancy on the day Germany invaded Belgium. Despite this, Ralph and Celia's brother Francis (who subsequently suffered acute shell-shock) rushed to enlist, with Ralph being sent to France around the same time as their daughter's birth in April 1915. Ralph was wounded in 1917 and awarded the DSO and bar in 1918. Both of Celia's daughters married the engraver Laurence Whistler.

MARY K GIBBONS

No information has been found.

SOPHIE PRESELY GLEMBY (1908-?)

No information has been uncovered, other than the fact that she was born in New York.

K M E GOTELEE (1891-1959)

Born in Islington, the second of three sisters; her father was a 'shop-walker' and draper's clerk. In the 1911 census she is listed as a 'student'. Like so many of her generation, she did not marry.

MURIEL ELSIE GRAHAM (1868-1928)

Born in Calcutta. Her justice of the peace father was an East India Company employee and her mother a vicar's daughter. By 1871 the family were living in Stirling, Scotland, where she appears to have remained throughout her life.

ALEXANDRA GRANTHAM (1868-1945)

By birth a German citizen, Alexandra almost certainly met her husband Frederick whilst they were both studying at Cambridge, she at Girton, where she achieved First Class Honours. A highly cultured woman, her pre-war writings reveal an early feminist/supporter of women's rights.

Frederick served in the Boer War and her writings of this period show a deep awareness of the emotional cost to women of having their husbands serving overseas. Subsequently a Reservist with the Royal Munster Fusiliers, Frederick served in France from September 1914. He was reported 'Missing' in May 1915 and only his dog-tag was found. Their son, Hugo, was a Regular Army officer in the Essex Regiment. In spring 1915 he embarked for Gallipoli.

Alexandra's lengthy elegy to Hugo, *Mater Dolorsa*, charts her grief work and internal conflict between wishing to accept that Hugo died an heroic death, yet realising she may be deluding herself. She also expresses anger with Frederick for having died when she needed him most. Her later war works reveal cleverly concealed anti-war sentiments, including the duping of the young by warmongers.

Hugo is buried at Twelve Tree Copse Cemetery, Gallipoli and Frederick is remembered on the walls at Le Touret. Alexandra's second son, Alexander, survived the War and became Governor of Hong Kong in the 1950s. Her much loved youngest son, Godfrey, was killed in June 1942; she also elegised him in verse.

JOAN GRIGSBY (née RUNDALL) (1892-1937)

Born in Dumfriesshire, her headmaster father was also a 'Clerk in Holy Orders'. In 1911 she was living with an aunt and uncle in Finchley, while working as a shorthand typist. She retained close ties with her beloved native Scotland, where she spent holidays. Her 1919 poetry collection *Peatsmoke and other verses* is dedicated to 'A. G.' – undoubtedly her husband Arthur Grigsby, a railway clerk with Great Eastern Railways, whom she married in 1912. They and their child emigrated to Canada in 1921.

'I. GRINDLAY', MARJORIE GRINDLEY (1899-1984)

Born in Cheshire, her father was founder of the W H Grindley Potteries company, which survived in various guises until 1991. She attended Moira House School in Eastbourne, and was undoubtedly better educated than many of her fellow WAACS. She served in the Edinburgh QMAAC. Her 1918 poetry collection *Ripples from the Ranks* was favourably reviewed in the *Aberdeen Journal*, 13 November 1918.

Her older brother Herbert was killed at Ypres in October 1915. Marjorie does not appear to have married and in 1923 gives her profession as 'None'. Sadly, according to the *Bath Chronicle and Weekly Gazette*, she was involved in a motor accident in Bath in early October 1927, when she killed a cyclist in heavy rain and gales. The coroner exonerated her from all blame and extended his sympathy to her, as well as to the family of the deceased young woman. Apart from her having crossed the Atlantic with her brother in 1922, no other information has been found about her life.

HELEN HAMILTON

Although relatively little is known about Schoolmistress Helen Hamilton, it is very probable that teaching was her work whilst mountaineering became her love. She climbed Mont Blanc in the early 1920s, having first travelled to the Alps for her health. The ironic style she employed in her war poetry is apparent across both her poetry and prose and either mountaineering or teaching informs all her writing. It appears as though she was a person who aroused strong emotions in those who knew her – not always positive ones.

MRS HAMILTON-FELLOWES

It is tempting to surmise from the 1911 census that she was the wife of a Church of England clergyman – her (written no later than 1915) 'Evening Hymn in Time of War' was subsequently published as a hymn. According to one contemporary critic, she 'is under no sentimental illusion as to the blessedness of war'. She also had a number of songs published during the War.

ADA LEONORA HARRIS (1860-1943)

Born in Surrey, Ada was the daughter of a broker's clerk. By 1911 she was living with her brother in Kingston-upon-Thames, giving her occupation as 'literary'. She wrote lyrics for several popular composers: 'In an Old-fashioned Town' (1914) was a significant 'hit' during the War. It is possible that seeing convoys of ambulances arriving at one of the two military and auxiliary hospitals in Kingston-upon-Thames prompted the poem. The most severely injured were often brought in under cover of darkness to avoid lowering civilian morale.

MARY HENDERSON (1875-1938)

Daughter of a Scottish architect living near Balmoral, the young Mary and her twin brother were invited to play with Queen Victoria's grandchildren. Unlike the monarch, she was a firm believer in women's suffrage and before the war was involved with many civic causes. When war broke out she became Honorary Secretary of the Dundee Women's War Relief Fund – a role she fulfilled admirably and she was associated with almost all of Dundee's war relief organisations. A request by her friend Dr Elsie Inglis to serve as Administrator of the Scottish Women's Hospital Units, transformed her life. Although at least one member considered her ill-suited to the role, a 'fat good natured Scot with no business capacity of any kind', this appears unfair. She remained in post, frequently crossing between Britain and Russia accompanying stores and supplies – her admiration for the nurses and doctors knew no bounds and was translated into her poetry. Like many SWH staff, she would undertake some nursing duties on the numerous occasions when the hospitals were inundated with casualties. She reached Petrograd from London on the day news of the Tsar's March 1917 abdication broke. By early summer 1917, she believed conditions in Russia were so hazardous that she advised the Foreign Office against any more women drivers being sent out to join the Unit. Some members, including SWH founder Dr Inglis, considered this close to treachery. However, this does not appear to have significantly damaged Inglis and Henderson's friendship. She died in November 1938 following what the *Aberdeen Journal* termed a 'mystery car crash' near Ballater. She fractured her skull, dying in the hospital on whose management committee she served. She was deeply mourned by the local community.

PAMELA HINKSON (1900-1982)

Daughter of Irish writer Katharine Tynan (q.v.). Her father became Resident Magistrate of County Mayo, Ireland, where the family lived from 1911. Pamela's adolescence was, like that of the majority of her generation, scarred by the War and she never married. She became a novelist and acted as secretary to her mother, whose extensive correspondence with the leading figures of Irish letters including W B Yeats, she also preserved. Whilst generally publishing under her own name, she took the pseudonym 'Peter Deane' for her Great War fiction.

PAULA HUDD

No information has been discovered about this poet. Her short stories were favourably reviewed during the War.

ELINOR JENKINS (1893-1920)

Born in India, Elinor's ancestors had a long record of public and military service. Her father was a high-ranking official in the Indian Civil Service, who played a significant role in moving the capital of India from Calcutta to Delhi. Her mother's family had served British interests in India for many generations. By 1901, as was not unusual amongst Anglo-Indian families, Mrs Jenkins was living in Devon with her five children whilst her husband remained overseas.

Elinor was educated at Southlands School in Fairfield, Exmouth, a small boarding-school 'for young ladies'; she was an able prize-winning scholar. During the War, she was one of several poets who worked for the intelligence services; there was no formal wartime interview process for women. They were simply expected to produce outstanding character references, be well-bred, reticent, ideally speak a foreign language, and be highly-educated – a profile she fitted perfectly.

Elinor's deeply loved uncle, Harry Spottiswood Trevor (b. 1889, Karachi), served on the Western Front and was killed on 15 August 1915. It is almost certainly her grief for him that permeates *Poems* (1916). Favourable reviews commented upon the outpouring of deep grief and love throughout the work. In 1917, her beloved elder brother Arthur transferred to the Royal Flying Corps and was killed on patrol duty in Yorkshire on 31 December 1917. Elinor and Arthur are both buried in Surrey. Her younger brother, Evan, became the last British governor of the Punjab and another brother, David, a Lord of Appeal.

MABEL JEFFREY (1884-1958)

Mabel was born in Stockbridge, Yorkshire into a family of steel producers originally making crinoline frames and then, as fashions changed, branching out into umbrella frames. By 1909, she was at Sheffield Union Hospital training as a nurse. The 1911 census gives her occupation as 'Nurse', but the fact that the nurses' relationship to the Head of Institution is 'Servant' speaks volumes about how nurses were viewed and treated. Mabel commented that despite paying steep fees trainee nurses were treated as 'cheap labour'.

She volunteered with the SWH at the Abbaye de Royaumont between March 1915 and March 1916 and latterly in Serbia. She also nursed with the French Flag Nursing Service. A niece inherited 'Auntie Mabel's' wartime memorabilia, which finally reached a wider audience in 1980. Her poem does not appear to have been published during the War but remained in the family's hands. Mabel went overseas black-haired in 1915 and, like a significant number of nurses, returned grey-haired in 1919, boasting both French and Serbian decorations.

HELEN KEY (1864-1946)

Born in Yorkshire. Her baronet husband was, like her father, a stockbroker. During the War she lived in Cornwall and several of her bellicose poems were published in local papers. She attracted considerable opprobrium from civilians and members of the Devon and Cornwall Light Infantry for her attitude towards Penzance workhouse's elderly residents, whom she referred to as 'Pampered Paupers' for being provided with fresh eggs – a luxury for civilians during the War.

Helen's jingoistic 'Hun-bashing' sentiments appear distasteful to twenty-first century readers but struck a chord during the War. She was quick to point a finger at 'shirkers', the term commonly used for men who did not enlist, whom she considered moral and physical cowards. Her work was widely reproduced in a number of local Australian newspapers, (including amongst others the *Kerang Observer* on Christmas Day 1915) apparently her 'views will strike a sympathetic note in many Australian women's hearts.' The Australian Government's proposals to introduce conscription never having been approved by the electorate, print and visual media were used to encourage Australian women to put pressure on men to enlist.

WINIFRED LETTS (1882-1972)

Her mother was Irish; her English clergyman father was a member of the Letts diaries publishing 'dynasty' (countless serving men and women kept diaries of their war service – frequently these were 'Letts diaries'). Pre-war, she had published two novels, a poetry collection, *Songs from Leinster* (1913) and had a play performed at Dublin's Abbey Theatre.

In 1915 VAD Letts joined the 2nd West General Hospital, Manchester before moving to Alnwick. An April 1916 edition of the *Alnwick Newspaper* reported that some '123 men are massaged every morning'; each masseuse saw between 30 and 40 patients daily. By January 1917, Letts was one of 3,388 masseurs and masseuses working with the Almeric Paget Military Massage Corps (APMMC), achieving her Medical Electricity Certificate in November 1917. By 1916, the APMMC was running the Massage Departments at all Military Hospitals, Command Depots and Convalescent Camps in the United Kingdom. Letts BRCS VAD record states that both her 'character' and her 'work' were 'very good'. Hospital work inspired much of her poetry.

Letts married a 67-year-old widower William Verschoyle in 1926, two of his three sons had been killed during the War. Widowed in 1944, she moved to Kent before returning to Ireland, where she died in 1972, having continued her writing career into the 1930s.

KATHLEEN LINDSAY (1876-1953)

Born in Gibraltar. From August 1915 to July 1918 she was a manageress at the Deptford Supply Reserve Depot, and a superintendent at Woolwich Arsenal, where she was in charge of approximately 1,200 staff. Like so many of her class, she almost certainly worked voluntarily. A Hayacinth Hunter kept a war diary of her time as a driver at the Arsenal and she mentions driving Lindsay around the huge factory complex. After the War, Lindsay returned to 'County' activities supporting events such as Girl Guide rallies and teachers' conferences.

ROSE MACAULEY (1881-1958) [Poem 'Picnic' not given]

One of six children, Rose Macauley, known as 'Emilie', spent much of her early childhood in Italy. She studied Modern History at Somerville College, Oxford, completing her studies in 1903. By 1906, she had achieved some fame with her first novel. In total, she published twenty-three novels and moved in literary circles which included Rupert Brooke.

Macauley worked initially as a VAD during the War, then on the land – which inspired a series of five poems. She joined the British propaganda Department and also shouldered responsibilities centred upon service exemptions and conscientious objectors. Her novel *Non-Combatants and Others* (1916) is highly critical of the War. Her flat, library and manuscripts were destroyed in a 1941 air raid. In 1958 she was made a Dame Commander of the British Empire (DBE).

HELEN MACKAY (1876–1966)

According to the *New York Times,* Helen Gansevoort Edwards was 'one of the prettiest girls in society' when she married wealthy New Yorker, Archibald Mackay in 1897. By 1914, she was living in France, writing prose sketches of French life. She worked throughout the War at the Hôpital St Louis in Paris. Her November 1915 visit to London provided material for her collection *London One November* and her prose text *Journal of Small Things.*

Post-war, she was awarded the Médaille de la Reconnaissance Française. A fluent French and Italian speaker, she published poetry and short stories as well as a novel in French. During World War Two, she became involved with social work and wrote two patriotic books about her adopted country.

ELLA FULLER-MAITLAND (1857–1939)

In the 1881 and 1911 censuses she gives her profession as author and indeed wrote extensively during these periods. Ella is absent from the 1891 and 1901 returns; her husband appears on none of them. It is possible that she was a semi-invalid, as an 1899 review of *The Etchingham Letters* (1895), comments that some of her depicted scenes are remarkable because 'they were written on an invalid's sofa in London.' The *English and European Authors Who's Who* in 1933 refers to her as living in Devon.

KATHERINE MANSFIELD [Beauchamp] (1888–1923)

Born in New Zealand, Katherine Mansfield was the daughter of a banker. She came to England in 1903 and studied at Queen's College, London, until she returned to New Zealand in 1906. When her father forbade her from becoming a professional cello player she returned to England in 1909, never re-visiting New Zealand.

The death of her much loved younger brother, Leslie Heron Beauchamp, 'Chummie', on 6 October 1915 was 'the greatest grief' of her life' and one from which Katherine never fully recovered. For a while she was unable to pursue her writing career due to her grief. Although it is impossible to be sure whether or not she knew this, Chummie's death was caused soon after his arrival on the Western Front when a defective grenade blew up in his hand; he and his sergeant were 'blown to bits'.

Eventually, needing to earn money, Katherine began to imagine that she was writing for 'Chummie'. However, she was diagnosed with tuberculosis in 1917. According to her second husband, John Middleton Murry, (from whom she separated after two weeks of marriage) 'no single one of Katherine Mansfield's friends who went to the War returned alive from it'. The couple were friendly with a number of the prominent authors of the day including Bertrand Russell, D H Lawrence, T S Eliot and Virginia Woolf.

She died in France of a pulmonary haemorrhage in January 1923.

'NINA MARDEL' (1887–1954)

Although cited in First Word War poetry bibliographies as a VAD, Mary Amelia Jose Mardel-Ferreiro Nina was in fact a professional nurse who had trained at the prestigious London Hospital. Her Portuguese father, an interpreter to the Admiralty, was a hopeless businessman and this may have encouraged Nina to enter nursing in order to gain financial independence.

An 'exemplary' nurse, she served (as Mary Ferreira) with the QAIMNS. In 1914, her 18-year-old brother Edmund was killed; another brother had already died of TB in 1910. Her third brother, Frank, survived the War. In 1916, she moved to the 'Palace of Pain', the military Royal Victoria Hospital at Netley – then the largest, longest building in England. Many poems in *Plain Song* reflect her nursing experiences and her religious faith.

In 1918, she married a former patient, John Fleming, who had been wounded and suffered with shrapnel in his lungs. Some of her poems hint at a shadowy romantic attachment, it is possible that, like many of her generation, she had suffered wartime bereavement. Nevertheless, the marriage appears to have been happy. In 1924, the family emigrated to Australia. Two of her three sons were killed in World War Two.

CONSTANCE LOUISA MAYNARD (1849–1935)

The first student from the female Girton College, Cambridge to study the Moral Sciences tripos, Maynard completed her studies in 1875 and taught at the prestigious Cheltenham Ladies' College. In 1880 she began studying at the London Slade School of Art, where she and a group of friends developed the idea of opening a Christian Women's College to prepare ladies for a University of London degree. In 1882 she became Mistress of Westfield College, subsequently a constituent college of the University of London. She retired in 1913, having taught some 500 women. Deeply religious, her writings included Divinity lectures as well as four volumes of war poetry, the first of which, according to her diary for 1914, 'despite many kind verdicts, fell flat'.

Poetry caused Maynard's first 'contact with the Law of the Land'. Her 1915 diary (digitised by Queen Mary University Library) recounts how her balanced

'Reply' to Ernst Lissauer's much publicised 'Hymn of Hate Against England', in which she expressed admiration of pre-war Germany and the Germans, was quoted out of context. Reprinted in 'the odious *John Bull*', she was mobbed, accused of being a pro-German spy and received hundreds of hate-mail letters. The War Office sent a 'courteous elderly policeman' to arrest her. Having read and discussed the poem with her, he left armed with copies of the piece, having agreed she was no spy.

A riot broke out in her village (Gerrard's Cross) where she sensed a 'cloud of evil' enveloping her. Although her lawyer told her to press charges against *John Bull's* editor, she let the matter drop. The following year, according to the local paper, she had another brush with authority because she was summoned to the Petty Sessions at Epsom for 'failing to reduce her drawing-room's lights.' She may still have felt unsafe, as some local residents had bayed for her blood. Her diaries show an elderly woman watching the War, lamenting the loss of young lives and aware that the cost in hatred, blood and treasure will be a burden to subsequent generations.

[KATHERINE] BEATRICE MAYOR (1885-1947)

One of ten children, Beatrice Meinertzhagen was a niece of social reformer Beatrice Webb. She was educated in London and Paris; in 1912 she married Robin Mayor, a philosopher who worked for the Board of Education. 'Spring 1917' appeared in her 1919 *Poems*, which started her literary career. She subsequently wrote several plays and two novels and her last poetry collection was published in 1943, making her one of several women to feature in bibliographies of both First and Second World War poetry.

In a letter to Vita Sackville-West, her friend Virginia Woolf describes Mayor as having 'gipsy blood in her: she's rather violent and highly coloured, sinuous too with a boneless body and thin hands'. Those hands may have been put to good use, as Mayor cut Woolf's hair short in February 1927.

ALICE MEYNELL (1847-1922)

Born in 1847 in Barnes, Surrey, the second daughter of Bohemian parents, Alice and her elder sister Elizabeth spent much of their childhood in Italy. Initially it was Elizabeth who, as Lady Butler, achieved considerable fame as a war artist. Queen Victoria purchased her famous painting 'The Roll Call', depicting the horrors of the Crimean War. Alice meanwhile had converted to Roman Catholicism and married impoverished Catholic journalist Wilfred Meynell in 1877.

She began to eclipse her artist sister, writing prolific columns for both middle-brow and religious publications and poetry praised by, amongst others, George Eliot. In 1892, following the poet laureate Alfred Lord Tennyson's death, her name was put forward for the laureateship; this re-occurred in 1913. Perhaps on this occasion her commitment to women's suffrage, as well as her gender, damned her in the nominating committee's eyes.

The War brought tragedy to the Meynells: one son-in-law, Percy Lucas, was killed on the Somme and her youngest son, Francis, was imprisoned as a conscientious objector in Hounslow Barracks. He collapsed, close to death, after ten days' hunger strike. *The Sunday Mirror* considered her a 'gentle poetess' and her work was read at 'Patriotic Poetry Readings', where proceeds were donated to various war charities.

E M MURRAY

No information has been found on Murray, other than her membership of the WAAC.

CAROLA OMAN CBE (1897-1978)

Born in Oxford, the second and younger daughter of military historian Sir Charles Oman; Carola aspired to being a writer from an early age. Denied the opportunity to attend boarding school and feeling that her education had been inadequate, she was determined to rise above its limitations.

She left school in the summer of 1914 and became a probationary VAD nurse at Oxford's Radcliffe Infirmary, subsequently working in London and Dorset before being sent to France in September 1918. She remained there until April 1919, working at rest stations in Boulogne, Wimereux and Terlingham. Carola was an acute poetic observer of the events following the Armistice and her service overseas provided her with material for *The Menin Road and other poems*, which she dedicated to four fellow VADs including her childhood friend May Wedderburn Cannan (q.v).

In a long writing career, she published fiction, history and biographies but it was for the latter for which she was renowned, winning *The Sunday Times* annual British literature prize for *Nelson* and the James Tait Black Memorial Prize for *Sir John Moore*. She married a war veteran in 1922.

[CATHERINE] EMILY ORR (1860-1937)

Daughter of a solicitor and later a vicar's wife, Emily had seven children. In the 1880s, the Society for Promoting Christian Knowledge published a number of her morally uplifting texts, including *Our Working Men and how to reach them*. In 1911, her family lived in Leicestershire.

EMILY PARKER (1863-1937)

Emily married a West Malling (Kent) 'jobbing gardener'. Like many young men, her youngest son, John had, at the age of seventeen, joined the Army Special Reserve of The Buffs, (East Kent Regiment). Still living at home, in February 1913, the idea of becoming a 'Saturday night soldier' must have seemed exciting, a welcome break from his job as a 'farm labourer'. A small lad, despite his medical history stating that he had 'slightly flat feet' and was 'slightly knock-kneed', he was mobilised on 8 August 1914 and killed on 3 August 1915. He is buried in Wulverghem–Lindenhoek Road Military Cemetery, Belgium, with sweeping views over the Messines Ridge – now a garden of tranquillity very different from its 1915 location as one of the most deadly positions on the Western Front.

JESSIE POPE (1868-1941)

Leicester-born, the daughter of a commercial traveller and hop merchant, Pope attended the North London Collegiate School for Girls where the school curriculum would have exposed her to significant amounts of poetry. An able scholar, she won a number of school prizes. From 1902 Jessie contributed prolifically to numerous periodicals and was recognised as both a writer of humorous verse and as a children's author. In 1911, she was living in Finchley.

From August 1914, she concentrated her writing efforts on patriotic, possibly jingoistic verses, which struck a chord with many of her readers. Her poetry was widely published, often to benefit causes and war charities, including St Dunstan's (for blind servicemen) where she volunteered and Great Ormond Street Children's Hospital. A number of her poems provide greater food for thought than titles such as *Simple Rhymes for Stirring Times* would suggest. In 1929, she married a retired bank manager and moved to Great Yarmouth.

DOROTHY UNA RATCLIFFE ('DUR') (1887-1967)

Sussex-born Dorothy spent her life in Yorkshire, following her 1909 marriage to Charles Ratcliffe, the nephew of Edward Brotherton, chemical millionaire and ultimately the benefactor of the Leeds University Brotherton Library. As Mayor of Leeds 1913-1914, the widowed Edward nominated Dorothy his Lady Mayoress – the youngest ever at the time.

When hostilities were declared, Edward offered to meet the cost of clothing and personally equipping the men of the embryonic Leeds Pals Battalion. The Mayor and Lady Mayoress watched the new recruits swearing their oath of allegiance at Leeds Town Hall in September 1914. On 1 July 1916, a battalion that had been 'two years in the making was', according to Leeds Pal Private A V Pearson, '10 minutes in the destroying' at Serre during the opening day of the Battle of the Somme.

French-speaking Dorothy also worked tirelessly for Leeds' Belgian refugees. Her sister's fiancé, her brother-in-law, Victor, with whom she had previously been romantically involved, was killed on 1 July 1916.

CONSTANCE ADA RENSHAW (1891-1964)

A Sheffield University graduate, Constance was also a talented actress, artist and sportswoman. In 1913, she began teaching, mainly at Sheffield City Grammar School and also at the Sheffield Teacher Pupil Centre; ill-health forced her retirement in 1937. A well-respected poet, her war poems were widely reproduced. Unusually, she also broadcast some of her poetry, including on Armistice evening 1925. Her writing won significant praise and indeed prizes during the War. 'The Lure of England' was awarded first prize for the best war poem in *Poetry Review* in November/December 1915, the first of a number of poetry prizes she received.

LADY MARGARET SACKVILLE (1881-1963)

Daughter of the 7th Earl de la Warr and a cousin of Vita Sackville-West, she became a well-respected poet in 1897, when her first collection was published. Like her mother, she was an active campaigner for women's suffrage and in 1900, commented that poetry was one of the few arenas in which women could engage on identical terms to men. Friendly with W B Yeats, she was elected Fellow of the Royal Society of Literature in May 1914.

Lady Margaret joined the Union of Democratic Control, which was founded in August 1914 to oppose the War and also counted the Labour leader, Ramsay Macdonald amongst its founding members. The anti-war *The Nation* published much of her poetry and her lengthy *The Pageant of War* (1916) received considerable critical acclaim. She was unafraid of pointing the finger of blame at those, including women and mothers, who allowed the War to happen and condoned its continuance.

She worked hard to alleviate the plight of Belgian refugees and throughout the War featured in newspaper society pages, interest in the aristocracy being keen in early twentieth century England. Her uncle, the 8th Earl, was a member of the Royal Naval Volunteer Reserve (RNVR); he died on 16 December 1915 following service in the Dardanelles. The title passed to his son, 16-year-old conscientious objector Herbrand, who finally agreed to serve in the Royal Naval Reserve (trawler section). He amazed his fellow Etonians, and the gentlemen of the Press, by enlisting as an able seaman as opposed to an officer. Herbrand was the first hereditary peer to support the Labour Party.

Despite having been engaged in 1909 to a man considered highly suitable, Margaret never married. She had a 16-year, passionate affair (lasting until 1929) with Ramsey Macdonald, the first Labour Prime Minister. She declined to marry him, however, largely because he was Presbyterian and she Roman Catholic. She became the first president of the Scottish PEN (the worldwide association of authors).

ETHEL TALBOT SCHEFFAUER (1888-1976)

In 1912 Londoner Ethel Talbot married Herman Scheffauer, the American-born son of a German immigrant father who had lived in Kensington for several years. Although trained as an architect, Herman was a minor poet, writer and translator of Thomas Mann's work. In May 1915, Ethel applied for an American passport as the couple were moving to Germany.

By 1921, they were living in Berlin with their daughter. *New Altars* (1921) was published by a Berlin press. It is anti-war and reconciliatory, seeking to 'bury the gods of war for only then can the world know peace'. According to The Bancroft Library, at the University of California, having murdered his secretary, 49-year-old Herman committed suicide in 1927. By 1939, Ethel and her daughter were living in Woolwich, South-East London, where she earned her living as a German/English translator until her death. Contrary to popular belief she is not the Ethel Talbot who was a prolific author of children's books.

AIMÉE BYNG SCOTT (1867-1953)

Born in India, Aimée was an Indian Army officer's daughter. By 1881, like so many such children, she, her mother and four siblings were living in England – her father may have remained overseas. In 1895, she too became an Indian Army wife through her marriage to Major-General Arthur Scott. He served on the Somme at Ovillers and also in the first great tank battle at Cambrai (1917). She wrote crime novels, appearing in *A Comprehensive Bibliography of Crime Fiction*.

MAY SINCLAIR (1863-1946)

By 1914, women's suffrage supporter May Sinclair was a respected author and friend of a number of the prominent literary figures of the day. Interested in Medico-Psychological Research, in psychoanalytic and psychic ideas, in 1914 she donated to a 'Fund for Nerve-Shocked Soldiers'. When she heard that an Ambulance Unit was being formed by an acquaintance, Hector Munro, she eagerly offered her services.

At this early stage, voluntary units were fighting each other to get to the war zone. May's 1915 *Journal of Impressions in Belgium* gives a vivid, if uncomplimentary, view of some early volunteers rushing hither and thither around London, desperate not to miss out on the war that would be 'over by Christmas'. She recognises that danger can be a magnet for both genders.

In September 1914, the Belgian Red Cross accepted the Hector Munro Ambulance Corps' offer of service: Sinclair and twelve other well-meaning individuals left for Ostend. Her ill-defined role included being keeper of the funds, a position for which she was, by her own admission, ill-suited. Her *Journal* reveals how painfully her dream of helping the wounded disintegrated. Whilst thousands of women found themselves admirably able to cope with what she refers to as the 'horror of bloody bandages and mangled bodies', May could not.

Despite the thrill of being in 'a military hospital under military orders', her short-comings soon became painfully apparent and she was eventually left floundering, 'feeling like a large and useless parcel which the Commandant had brought with him in sheer absence of mind, and was now anxious to lose or otherwise get rid of.'

Unceremoniously returned to England, she published her *Journal* and poems demonstrating admiration for those who were able to deal with the horrors and chaos of the early weeks of the War, and bitterness towards those who had taken advantage of the money she had given to the Unit, gone overseas, and successfully stolen her 'dream' from her. Her sense of rejection runs counter to much uniformed women's poetry, which frequently celebrates women's commitment to the cause they themselves visibly represent. She was deeply aware of and concerned for the plight of Belgium and her citizens and the fate that awaited them at the hands of the advancing Germans.

MARJORIE KANE SMYTH (D.1936?)

An Australian, Marjorie lived in New South Wales; her father may have been a clergyman because in 1904 she passed Junior examinations at a Clergy Daughters' School in New South Wales. She was one of the earliest Australians to volunteer as a VAD, arriving in Egypt on 12 October 1915; some ninety-two Australian women served in this capacity. She worked at No. 1 Australian General Hospital, 'Heliopolis Palace' a huge complex which, according to the Hospital's own records, was in 'the land of the Pharaohs' as a 750-bed hospital from January 1915 to March 1916. Marjorie would have cared for patients from Gallipoli.

The hospital then transferred to France, with bed capacity increasing to 1,040, and Marjorie served there until June 1917. She was awarded the 1914-1915 Star as well as the British War and Victory medals. She may have died around 1935, as that is the last year she appears on the NSW electoral roll.

VIOLET SPENDER (née Schuster) (1878-1921)

The only daughter of a German-born barrister father, Violet was close to her brothers and grieved deeply when her brother Alfred was killed in November 1914; his name is on the Menin Gate. Following Violet's own death in December 1921, her husband collected and published her poems in *The Road to Caister*. Just as poetry was a form of grief work for her during the War, compiling the collection was 'a sacred task' for her widower, who took comfort from her last words, "I have had a happy life."

In his Foreword, Harold Spender explains how Violet 'wrote poetry because she could not help it.' Although poetry was often fun for her, Harold selected 'graver poems inspired by the events she lived through for the last ten years of her life. The Great War filled her mind with deep perplexities: She looked out on its waste and desolation with agonising pity for all men: and like many of her generation, she often sought relief in poetry.' Their son, Sir Stephen Spender, became a key literary figure in the Modernist movement.

M STONE

No personal information has been located. Members of the Women's Volunteer Reserve would have been predominantly middle/upper class, if for no other reason than the uniform which, according to the organisation's newsletter cost £2 (around £180 in 2016), had to be paid for out of personal pockets, placing it out of poorer women's reach. The skirts were intended to be 'serviceable and sensible, and could be worn at any time.' Members spent considerable amounts of time drilling, as the Corps' objective was to create a body of disciplined women to act as dispatch riders, signallers, telegraphists, motorists, and trench diggers who nevertheless remained 'womenly women not second-class men'.

MURIEL STUART (1885-1967)

Born in London, Muriel's barrister father had Scottish ancestry. Hugh Macdiarmid considered her the 'best poet' of the inter-war Scottish Renaissance', whilst Thomas Hardy called her poetry 'superlatively good'. In 1926, American editor Henry Savage went so far as to say that with 'Alice Meynell being dead, there is no English poet living today who is Muriel Stuart's peer.'

Nonetheless, her wide-ranging poetry is now largely forgotten. As well as writing poetry with a religious theme, both during and after the War, she poetically addressed the violation of women in the Occupied Areas of France and Belgium, and also the opprobrium heaped upon women who gave birth to 'bastards'. During the War she worked for publishers Herbert Jenkins and also Heinemann (see publishers section). In 1921, she became a founder member of PEN to promote literature and freedom of expression. Her post-war poetry explored the need for equal partnerships between men and women.

SARA TEASDALE (1888-1933)

A prolific, critically acclaimed American poet, Sara was part of the poetry circle surrounding the American *Poetry* magazine edited by Harriet Monroe. In 1918 she was awarded the Columbia University Poetry Society Prize, subsequently renamed the Pulitzer Prize for Poetry. Having suffered bouts of depression and lived as a semi-invalid following her divorce in 1929, she committed suicide with an overdose of barbiturates in 1933. Her wartime poetry, whilst retaining the lyrical voice commented upon by critics, shows a deep awareness of the travesties of war.

[Alice] EVELYN TOLLEMACHE (1872-1941)

One of eight children, Alice's younger brothers, Harold and Lyonel served during the War and both survived. In the 1911 census she does not give a profession and *The New Crucifixion* appears to be her only published collection of poetry.

SARAH TOYE (1869-1951)

On the 1901 census, Sarah's semi-literate husband gives his occupation as a shipyard worker. By 1911, she was a widow with seven children living in Londonderry. Her eldest son was a baker, whilst two other sons are listed on the census as 'cabinet makers'. Her son John, known as Vincent to his family, enlisted with the Royal Iniskillings Fusiliers early in the War. He was killed in Gallipoli on 2 July 1915 and, like countless others of the ill-fated campaign, he has no grave; his is one of the 20,878 names inscribed on the towering Helles Memorial.

ALYS FANE TROTTER (1863-1961)

Born in Ireland. In 1886 she married civil engineer Alexander Pelham Trotter, editor of *The Electrical Magazine*. The couple lived with their young daughter and son in South Africa between 1896 and 1898, as Alexander was electrical advisor to the Cape Colonial Government. She published and illustrated a book about the Old Cape, which the family had explored by bicycle. Upon returning to England, Alexander became electrical advisor to the Board of Trade and Alys contributed prose and poetry to middle-brow periodicals.

Nigel and Other Verses (1918) is dedicated to her 20-year-old Regular Army Officer son, who was killed near Béthune on 12 October 1914. On the family's return from South Africa, she appears to have divided her time between Fittleworth in Sussex and London, ending her days in Wiltshire.

KATHARINE TYNAN (1861-1931)

A renowned and prolific Irish writer and poet, Katharine was closely involved with the Irish Revival. W B Yeats proposed to her in 1891, but she was secretly engaged to classical scholar, Henry Hinkson whom she married in 1893. They settled in London where their two sons and daughter Pamela (q.v.) were born. Tynan's writing successfully supported the family. In 1911, mainly through 'networking', she acquired the position of Resident Magistrate for County

Mayo for her now lawyer husband and the family returned to Ireland remaining there throughout the War.

Her wartime poetic output was considerable: she wrote condolence poems for bereaved friends, personalising these with details of their dead sons' life. Belief in the holiness of the War underpins all her poetry, soldiers are New Crusaders. With her sons serving with the Royal Irish Regiment in Gallipoli and France (they survived), she could empathise with mothers' fears and anguish.

Widowed in 1919, her sight, which had started to fail her at the age of seven, deteriorated to near-blindness. She died of cerebral thrombosis in April 1931 and is buried in Kensal Green Cemetery, close to her friend Alice Meynell (q.v.). Although her poetry has fallen out of favour, during much of the War it struck the right chord with the public and received considerable critical acclaim.

MARGARET TYRRELL-GREEN (1863-1942)

Her husband, the Reverend Edmund Tyrrell-Green was Professor of Hebrew and Theology at St David's College, Lampeter (now the University of Wales). He wrote widely on Christian doctrine and Church architecture as well as, unusually for a father at the time, a text that explores paternal grief.

Their Cambridge educated elder son, Denis (b.1894) volunteered in September 1914, being commissioned Lieutenant with the Royal Sussex Regiment. He survived the Gallipoli campaign, where, according to De Ruvigny's Roll of Honour, he was commended by the General Commanding the Division for doing valuable reconnoitring and map-drawing work.' Invalided home, he returned to action in Egypt and Palestine. He was killed on 26 March 1917 at El-Shelluf and is commemorated on the Jerusalem Memorial, Jerusalem War Cemetery, as well as on three UK War memorials. Denis's Padre wrote of a delightful, devout young officer whose men referred to him as 'splendid'.

More Poems is dedicated to 'my son Denis in gratitude for a loving and lovely life laid down in the service of God and of his country.' One touching piece composed in memory of a friend's sons, brothers Duncan and Gwion Bowen Lloyd, who were killed in Gallipoli within a week of each other in August 1915, appeared in *The Cambrian* on 15 February 1916.

VIVIANE VERNE (1864-1921)

The only known piece of information about Viviane is she also published lyrics during the War. In the *Western Daily Press* of 14 August 1916, the music reviewer felt that there was 'tenderness and simple expression' in her 'We Cannot Forget'.

ALBERTA VICKRIDGE (1890-1963)

One of three sisters born into a strict Methodist household, as a young child, Alberta's literary talent was already apparent. By 1914 she was establishing a name for herself in the local literary and art worlds. Due to their mother's ill-health, the family frequently left their native Yorkshire and holidayed in Devon.

In 1914 VAD Vickridge joined the Red Cross Town Hall Hospital in Torquay. Like hospitals across the land, it published its own magazine often featuring her poetry. VAD Agatha Christie was the magazine editor. Almost fanatical about poetry, Vickridge confessed to reading 'poetry when she ought to be asleep and dream[ing] it when she ought to be awake!' She won several poetry prizes. Arguably, her most significant achievement occurred in January 1918 when her 'Out of Conflict' won first prize in a *Poetry Review* competition for the 'Best Poem' by a poet On Active Service whilst the now world-renowned war poet Wilfred Owen came second with 'Song of Songs'.

She continued to win poetry competitions post-war and also edited *The Jongleur* a quarterly magazine of verse, as well as publishing several collections of poetry, including one in World War Two.

JESSIE WAKEFIELD (1881-1946)

Born in Barnsley, her father was a surveyor and sanitary inspector. Her husband Edward was a buyer with the Co-operative Stores in Barnsley and it is tempting to surmise that they met in the town, as they married in 1909, two years after his arrival there. During the War a few of Jessie's pieces were published in magazines such as the *Westminster Gazette*. Post-war, she had two volumes of poetry published, one edited by Alberta Vickridge (q.v.) as well as several humorous sketches 'for co-operators' and she was closely involved with the Co-operative movement.

KATHLEEN MONTGOMERY WALLACE (1890-1958)

The daughter of a Cambridge lecturer in Mathematics, Kathleen's twin sister died in infancy. Educated at the Perse School, Cambridge and at Girton College, she achieved a degree in English in 1914. Her brother Basil Coates was killed in 1915 and he is remembered on the Ploegstreet Memorial.

She wrote for a number of women's magazines as well as novels and poetry. Her elegiac war poems published in *Lost City, Verses* explore her sense of a doomed world and the War's devastating effects on her generation and on Cambridge itself. In February 1917 she married Major James Hill Wallace, OBE, (attached to the Canadian Mounted Rifles). With their four sons they lived first in Canada and then China (which provides the backdrop for a number of her adult novels), before returning to England in 1927. She also wrote children's fiction.

WINIFRED WEDGWOOD (1874-1963)

Born in Bayswater, London, Winifred was the daughter of a stocks and shares dealer. By 1911, she and her widowed mother lived in Tunbridge Wells, looked after by a live-in cook and housemaid; neither states a profession in the census. In the Foreword to *Verses of a VAD Kitchen-Maid*, Wedgwood acknowledges that the inspiration for many of her poems was the 'Military Hospital Kitchen' where she served as a kitchen-maid with the Devonshire 26th VAD, the same hospital as Agatha Christie and Alberta Vickridge (q.v.).

Wedgwood was undoubtedly a General Service VAD (GSVAD). This corps was formed in 1915 to assume jobs previously performed by men in military hospitals, thereby freeing up men for the Front. Kitchen work was considered the lowest form of service and many VAD nurses looked down on kitchen-maids. GSVADs served in all theatres, ran the same risks as nurses and occasionally died as a result of their service. These generally less articulate VADs have almost faded out of memory.

LUCY WHITMELL (1869-1917)

The daughter of a justice of the peace and magistrate, Lucy Whitmell lived in Leeds. One of her seven sisters was a member of the Army Nursing Reserve. Her much older husband was a retired inspector of schools. Her poem 'Christ in Flanders' was widely quoted in sermons by the Bishop of London (Padre of the London Rifle Brigade) Winnington-Ingram, and the Archbishop of York. The poem was available in leaflet form and, according to *The New Outlook*, by 9 August 1916 nearly 50,000 copies (cost 6d for 50 copies) had been sold. It was reprinted in New York City at the Chapel of the Comforter, in Horatio Street, as Gospel Leaflet No. 11, and was widely distributed in card form, as well as being set to music post-war.

The Publishers

'If you have words - / Fit words'
(Helen Hamilton)

Poets might have words, but if they are to be heard they need to be published. It is often impossible to know why a poet chose, or indeed was chosen, by a particular publishing house. Although many of the firms that published poetry during the War have undergone multiple take-overs, disappeared or are untraceable, some information is available about others. The stories and snippets that have been uncovered are integral to our understanding of women war poets, the war poetry genre and its unique place in English literature.

Despite understandable pessimism when war broke out, the book trade did not initially see a decline in either sales or in the availability of paper, much of which was, by 1914, imported. The situation deteriorated from late 1915 and by December 1917, shipping priorities were 'Food, Munitions or Men'. Although wood-pulp clearly did not fit into any of these categories, publishers wondered if they could claim preferential treatment as books were 'of national importance'. In this way the industry was simply echoing sentiments expressed from early on in the War, as books (including collections of poetry) had been constructed as part of the 'war effort'. It was felt that suitably patriotic texts reminded servicemen and women of what they were fighting to preserve and helped to maintain morale, so huge numbers were sent to troops overseas; cheap imprints were established for war workers and troops, and posters and charities pleaded for funds to purchase books for soldiers.

What follows is in no way a comprehensive list, simply an overview of a few of the publishers active during the First World War and the poets they published:

ANDREW MELROSE: Helen Mackay

Andrew Melrose began publishing in 1899. In the early years of the twentieth century, he both published and contributed to *Boys of the Empire*, the official paper of the Boys' Empire League whose aim was 'to promote and strengthen a worthy Imperial Spirit in British-born boys'. Despite these rather Establishmentarian ideas, Melrose was not afraid of controversy and in 1915 he published Welsh author Caradoc Evans' *My People*, a shocking portrayal of poverty in Wales.

B H BLACKWELL: May Wedderburn Canaan; Eleanor Farjeon; Helen Hamilton

Having opened a bookshop in Oxford in 1879, bookseller Benjamin Blackwell moved into publishing in 1897, his one aim being to promote access to literature for poorer people. The Blackwell family had roots in the Temperance movement, which promoted self-education and reading as well as teetotalism. Blackwell's produced cheaper editions of Shakespeare and popular novels. According to the firm's own history, customers and visitors to the shop were welcome 'to scrutinise and handle the books on the shelves without obligation to buy'. In 1915, Blackwell's published Tolkein's first poem, 'Goblin's Feet'.

BODLEY HEAD: Helen Parry Eden, Dorothy Una Ratcliffe

So named for the founder of the Oxford Bodleian Library – the firm had a head of Sir Thomas Bodley as its insignia and a bust of him above the shop door. In 1887, Elkin Mathews and John Lane had started a joint publishing venture, Bodley Head, to produce works 'of stylish decadence' as well as the *belles-lettres* of the *fin-de-siècle*, including Oscar Wilde. The partnership was short-lived, as Elkin Mathews left in 1894 to set up his own house. Both before and during the War, Bodley Head published several young poets and also many mainstream authors including, post-war, Agatha Christie.

BURNS AND OATES: Alice Meynell; Alys Fane Trotter

Established in 1835, the house faced collapse when the owner, James Burns, converted to Catholicism in 1847; however assistance from Cardinal Newman, who chose the firm as his publisher, helped it survive. Alice Meynell's husband Wilfred became literary advisor and manager at the house in the 1870s. According to Wilfred's 1948 obituary, 'beautifully printed books (for the first and last time) issued from a Catholic publisher'. The Meynells moved into the empty disused top floor of Burns and Oates's London premises, which had a lift that deposited visitors in the bathroom. In 1913 Burns and Oates became even more closely connected to the Meynells, as their son Francis (subsequently a conscientious objector), began working there. Due to his interests, high standards of typography were soon noticeable.

CONSTABLE & CO LTD: Celia Furse, Katherine Mansfield

Founded in 1795 by Edinburgh resident Archibald Constable, the firm published Sir Walter Scott as well as Bram Stoker's *Dracula*. Generous to authors, in 1813 Constable was the first publisher to offer an advance on royalties and in 1825 began to publish mass-market high-quality literature. Closed due to bankruptcy in 1826, the firm re-opened the following year and remained in business. In 1921 Constable became the first publisher to advertise on the London Underground.

C W DANIEL: Elsie Paterson Cranmer; S Gertrude Ford

Established in 1902, C W Daniel had links with the firm that had the agency for Tolstoy's writing. Daniel wanted to make the thoughts of the world's greatest thinkers affordable for the common man; he sold these so cheaply it is unlikely that he made a profit. A pacifist and a vegetarian, the name he initially chose for one of the magazines he published, *The Crank*, must have appeared to many in Edwardian times to reflect its owner's tendencies.

Daniel was twice prosecuted under the terms of the Defence of the Realm Act (DORA) for publishing pacifist works. His refusal to pay the £80 fine led to his being imprisoned for two months. Perhaps not anticipating wide sales, authors (and presumably poets) were asked to subsidise or even pay the costs of publishing. Some had to guarantee to buy a certain number of copies. This would indicate that the women he published enjoyed at least some financial independence.

CHATTO & WINDUS: Helen Dircks

Founded in 1855. By 1914, minor poet E Windus was a partner. The firm had a prestigious list of authors including Mark Twain, W S Gilbert, Wilkie Collins, H G Wells, Richard Aldington, and it also handled the first translation of Marcel Proust's *A La Recherche du Temps Perdu*.

ELKIN MATHEWS: Kathleen Braimbridge; Helen Key

Considered an important figure in London literary life at the turn of the nineteenth and twentieth centuries, Mathews' list included W B Yeats (who soon left him), Lionel Johnson, James Joyce and Ezra Pound. According to a 1992 review of *Elkin Mathews: Publisher to Yeats, Joyce, Pound*, he was a timid individual – apparently he would go rushing for the 'cellar privy' when certain female customers arrived in his shop. He nevertheless gave evidence at the Oscar Wilde trials. Although cautious by nature, he could also make bold publishing decisions and he instigated two cheap poetry series.

Known for his meanness when dealing with authors, he struggled post-war to adapt to the modernist winds of change blowing through the literary world.

ERSKINE MACDONALD: Madeleine Bedford; Sybil Bristowe; Vera Brittain; Mary Collins; S Gertrude Ford; I Grindlay; Mary Henderson; Nina Mardel; Constance Renshaw; Alberta Vickridge

Erskine Macdonald became, according to *London Opinion*, the 'unofficial publisher to the poets of the British Army' and indeed to many of the women poets of the War. The firm's far from scrupulous behaviour provides insights into the wave of poetry and desire for publication that was sweeping the land at the time. Would-be poets of both genders were encouraged to submit work to 'Macdonald' which, for a fee of half a crown (about £12 in 2015), would be critiqued, but only if the aspiring poet also subscribed to the firm's series *Little Books of Georgian Verse*. The ploy worked and significant numbers of poets were drawn into his net.

At least on some occasions, Erskine Macdonald published at the expense of the author or their family and paid royalties slowly, if at all. He may have worked on the premise that for at least some of his authors, or their parents, getting published was more important than any money they might earn. Many amongst the publishing fraternity considered his methods abhorrent.

Erskine Macdonald was not averse to taking what we would now call 'sweeteners' from would-be authors. In 1918, Vera Brittain's father, a paper manufacturer, offered Erskine Macdonald ten reams of antique printing paper. Brittain was probably not alone in becoming increasingly frustrated by the delays in publication of her *Verses of a VAD*. Sadly, in her case the delay was such that her brother Edward who had followed the progress of the collection with interest, was killed two months before it finally appeared. The situation may not have been unique. Erskine Macdonald published S Gertrude Ford's *Poems of War and Peace*, which was sold in aid of the British Red Cross Society.

HEFFER: Mary Boyle; Kathleen Wallace

William Heffer was the son of a Suffolk agricultural labourer who worked in Cambridge as a groom. Having been loaned a small sum of money, he set up business as a stationer, then subsequently a bookseller in Cambridge and by 1898, he had moved into publishing. Cheap textbooks for undergraduates became a hallmark of the business. Five of his nine children became actively involved in the business, which survived for 100 years.

HEINEMANN: Enid Bagnold; Mary Borden; Alexandra Grantham

Founded by William Heinemann in 1890; his father came originally from Hanover in Germany. By the turn of the century, Heinemann's list included Rudyard Kipling, Robert Louis Stevenson and H G Wells. It is interesting to speculate that Heinemann's Germanic roots may have attracted German-born Alexandra Grantham. Heinemann had been at the Book Trade Fair in Germany when war broke out.

Despite his nephew and heir serving in the British Army, his German name made him a target for the anti-German wave of hatred sweeping the land and his London office was pelted with rubbish and horse manure. Unlike a number of British citizens with German antecedents (including the Royal Family), he decided against Anglicising his name. The firm's output remained 'patriotic' although it attracted the attention of the censors. Heinemann published Robert Graves and Siegfried Sassoon's first collections (both authors had Germanic roots) and he became friendly with Sassoon. Proud of his German heritage, Heinemann was nevertheless an outspoken critic of German atrocities, including the August 1914 destruction of the library at Louvain in Belgium.

METHUEN & CO: Muriel Stuart

Teacher Algernon Methuen founded the firm in 1889 as a way of producing and marketing his own textbooks. He believed in books that were 'helpful' and early publications were predominantly non-fiction, academic works. In 1892, Methuen published Rudyard Kipling's *Barrack-Room Ballads*. The firm grew rapidly and began to encourage female authors. Charged with obscenity after publishing D H Lawrence's *The Rainbow* (1915), Methuen agreed to destroy all remaining copies following two police visits to their premises on 3 November 1915. This might, according to Iain Stevenson in *Book Makers – British Publishing in the Twentieth Century*, have stemmed from Lawrence's far from generous portrait of the chief editor's brother who had recently been killed.

SIDGWICK AND JACKSON: Elinor Jenkins, Violet Spender, Katharine Tynan

Founded in 1908, it was considered one of the premier publishing houses of the War. Katharine Tynan in *The Bookman* (October 1916) wrote that 'Sidgwick and Jackson's name on a volume of poetry is nearly always a guarantee of the quality'. They published a number of Tynan's collections, as well as works by Rose Macauley, Rupert Brooke and several other male poets.

SIMPKIN, MARSHALL, HAMILTON, KENT AND CO: Viviane Verne

This firm originated before 1814 under a Benjamin Crosby; Simpkin and Marshall were his assistants. During the mid–nineteenth century the firm was England's largest book wholesaler. In about 1890-1891, it expanded to become Simpkin, Marshall, Hamilton, Kent and Company with a wide publishing remit.

STOCKWELL: Eva Dobell; Olive Downes; Evelyn Tollemache

Established in 1898, it is still run by the great-grandchildren of the founder, Arthur Stockwell having moved from London to Devon, after being bombed during the Second World War.

THACKER, SPINK & CO.: Aimée Byng Scott

Set up in Bombay by William Thacker in the 1830s, by 1914, the firm was based in Calcutta. Unsurprisingly, they published a number of Anglo–Indian writings and writers including Rudyard Kipling, who carried on a lengthy correspondence with them in the 1880s.

Publications:

The Bookman

A monthly literary periodical devoted to 'Book buyers, Book readers and Book sellers.' Established in 1891, it was a middlebrow publication, priced at 6d, about the same cost as a 1914 4lb (1.8kg) loaf of bread; 'aspirational readers' with limited disposable income could afford to buy a copy. It had featured some of J M Barrie and W B Yeats' early works and always contained book reviews, poems, literary criticism and features on authors.

The Englishwoman

This monthly journal cost one shilling with about the same as 4lb (2kg) of sugar in 1914 was intended to 'reach the cultured public and bring before it in a convincing and moderate form the case for the Enfranchisement of Women'. The articles were generally but not exclusively on 'women's topics' and most editions during the War included at least one poem, not all with war themes. Its September 1914 edition assured readers that the publication 'will endeavour to represent the opinion of the large number of women who feel the full horrors of the War, who ardently desire peace, but who yet would not buy it at the price of honour.' The range of poems it published largely reflect this view.

Herald

By August 1914 the previously *Daily Herald* only appeared weekly. Firmly anti-war, it played a key role in the anti-conscription campaigns and supported conscientious objectors. Throughout the War, it unsurprisingly published pacifists' work. In 1917 it supported the Russian Revolution and was never averse to publishing articles showing the particular burdens war was placing on the poor. Alice Meynell's pacifist son Francis was on the editorial board.

The Nation

Despite starting life in 1907 as a Liberal publication, during the War, it became a Labour one. Its editor H V Massingham, a member of the Union for Democratic Control, used it to campaign for peace. Post-war, it attacked the economic policies of Stanley Baldwin and the Conservative Government. In 1930, it merged with *The New Statesman* and as *The New Statesman and The Nation* earned the reputation of being the country's leading intellectual weekly.

Westminster Gazette

Initially a daily, subsequently evening liberal broadsheet first published in 1893; it used distinctive light green paper. Poems by many revered poets, as well as unknowns, appeared in the *Gazette*. With its sister paper, *Saturday Westminster Gazette*, it was 'an organ of wide intellectual interests and sound taste in all the arts' *(The Spectator)*. Gender-blind, it offered a weekly 'Prize Poem' competition on wide-ranging topics. Some were home-based, others for men and women on active service, sometimes parodies were suggested, on other occasions a 'Latin or Greek tag'. During the War, its circulation was not particularly wide but it was seen as influential. It merged with the *Daily News* in 1918 and ceased publication in 1928.

(Edward) Lawrence Levy 1851–1932 (Scrapbook Compiler)

Lawrence Levy was a prominent member of the Birmingham Jewish community. Born in London, in 1891 at the age of forty he won the first British Amateur Weightlifting Championship. He also acted as a weightlifting judge in the 1896 Olympic Games. He was a pioneering teacher, and newspaper reporter. When war broke out, he became a leading theatrical impresario directing the Birmingham Athletic Club in a three-year campaign to entertain wounded soldiers in the suburban military hospitals. He encouraged members of the Birmingham Athletic Group to undertake voluntary work at weekends in munitions factories. He was the founder of the Amateur Gymnastics Federation of Great Britain and Ireland.

The Birmingham War Poetry Scrapbooks Collection

'Everybody's Aunt Lucy and Uncle George has written something'
(Ezra Pound)

No serious student of World War One poetry should overlook this unique collection, which corroborates Ezra Pound's much-quoted statement. In December 1918, Walter Powell, Chief Librarian of Birmingham Public Library, began placing advertisements in local, national and international newspapers requesting readers to submit a poem or poems that they had written during the War. He specified that these should have been written as 'private expressions' or published only in 'ephemeral' form, such as broadsides or postcards.

The response was overwhelming; poems flooded in from across the English-speaking world. Letters often accompanied the submission and these provide a fascinating background to the poet, the poem's composition and the universality of poetry. One mother admitted that she had written and sent her son a poem every day during the time he was overseas. Other writers alluded to personal and financial hardship now being endured; more than one impoverished war widow hoped to receive some small remuneration for her poem. Frustratingly, Powell left no record of his criteria for selecting the poems he retained, or any indication of whether compassion influenced his choice, but he was undoubtedly gender blind.

At the same time as collecting and collating the handwritten poems which run to four large scrapbooks, Powell became the beneficiary of 'The War Poetry Collection', consisting of 1,233 printed volumes written by canonised poets, by unknown soldiers, by civilians and by women. These were donated in 1921 by William John Cross (about whom nothing further is known) in memory of Private William John Billington, the son of a Birmingham cabinet maker born in 1897. The young soldier served with the London Regiment in France, Salonika and Egypt and was killed in action, in Palestine in 1918. Placed alongside the handwritten poems, the collection of printed volumes, which

Powell continued to add to through donations and purchases, grew over many decades.

The jewel in the crown of the Birmingham collection is the 'scrapbook collection'. As well as the four scrapbooks containing the responses to Powell's requests, there are five compiled by a Gladys Perhson, two scrapbooks which form the Lawrence Levy bequest and finally forty-four huge volumes entitled *A Collection of Poems Relating to the European War 1914-1918 from Newspapers, Magazines etc.* All the scrapbooks present the researcher with problems but none more so than the forty-four volume set. The volumes are un-paginated but in total run to over 3,000 pages, often with up to ten poems pasted on each page. The particular challenges they present relate to the quantity and legibility of the poems, as well as the sheer number of volumes. Clippings are undated and unattributed. Sometimes a poem appears under the poet's initials in one publication, anonymously or their full name is given in another. It is often impossible to know if the cutting is duplicated or from a different publication and, with the passing of time, there are now significant preservation issues. Old glue and 'crinkly' paper make reading some poems frustratingly hard and occasionally the compiler cut off the end of or even an entire line.

What becomes obvious on even a superficial glance through the material is that once again, the gender of the poet was irrelevant. In a poem published in *The Egoist* (December 1914), Herbert Blenheim ruefully declared, 'At the sound of the drum/Oh Tommy, they've all begun to strum.' Just occasionally, when grappling with these scrapbooks, even the most enthusiastic researcher is forced to admit that they wish the strumming had been more restrained.

The volumes of poetry, the preserved letters, and, perhaps above all, the scrapbooks that flooded in to Birmingham in response to Powell's appeal (which continued into the early 1920s) demonstrate that this was and has remained the most literary war ever fought. It was fought not primarily by the intelligentsia but by very ordinary men and women, such as Cadbury's employee Elsie Mewis, who told Walter Powell that although she was 'only a factory worker' she had written and sold poems to benefit 'our Tommies [and] Belgian refugees'. She shared with him her pride in having been able to 'help a little' in her country's 'hour of need'.

Elsie was perhaps less aware that her poems and those of the hundreds of other women who expressed in verse their hopes, fears, excitement, grief and despair over four long years were inadvertently creating an unparalleled resource for understanding women's war, women's lives and women's history.

Index

Poems